Joyful Noise

Order this book online at www.trafford.com
or email orders@trafford.com

Most Trafford titles are also available at major online book retailers.

Note for Librarians: A cataloguing record for this book is available from Library
and Archives Canada at www.collectionscanada.ca/amicus/index-e.html

Printed in Victoria, BC, Canada.

ISBN: 978-1-4269-0793-7 (sc)
ISBN: 978-1-4269-0795-1 (eb)

*Our mission is to efficiently provide the world's finest, most comprehensive book publishing
service, enabling every author to experience success. To find out how to publish your book, your
way, and have it available worldwide, visit us online at www.trafford.com*

Trafford rev. 09/24/09

North America & international
toll-free: 1 888 232 4444 (USA & Canada)
phone: 250 383 6864 ♦ fax: 812 355 4082

INTRODUCTION

I like to laugh and hope you do too. This book was inspired by a really funny joke I heard many years ago. I had trouble remembering it the next day but I tried telling it anyway and ruined the punch line (do you know the feeling?).

To avoid ruining any more good jokes I kept joke notes to help me remember and retell my favorites. I even started looking for new jokes to share but after checking the library and several bookstores I couldn't find a source book for good spiritual jokes.

So to fill this void I've put together my own volume of the best jokes and puns that I could find and keep them tied to a spiritual and Christian theme (some loosely).

I have included some very old jokes and puns that may seem tired to the reader but which still make me smile. This is the standard I felt I had to apply in deciding what to include - that which I still found funny.

My personal tastes will not be shared by all. I have made an effort to exclude the profane, obscene and overtly tasteless. But I still find there is a remaining undercurrent of irreverence and indelicacy that may bother some readers. I kept this material anyway because I have come to believe that taking ourselves and God too seriously can be limiting to our growth as true Christians.

I believe this volume is in keeping with a Christian ideal that is consistent with peace, love and joy.

But if you think the material has gone too far astray or becomes inappropriate to your own beliefs in any way, please look for a way to change or use it in a way that is more appealing. It is almost always our choice of language that causes separation and discord. The nice thing about words is that they can be flexible within the bounds of the mind that reads and uses them. Continue to use yours wisely.

Humor, at it's best, breaks down many of the barriers that seem to separate us from each other. A shared laugh calls for no response and lets the heart open to join with others at a deeper level.

I hope that you find a laugh or more within this volume. Please enjoy and share it. And if any story or expression bothers you too much, just rip it out and stomp on it!

The world is yours to create!

TABLE OF CONTENTS

OUR MINISTER

TALKING BACK

A man is walking across the street next to the church and is hit by a speeding van. Our minister comes out of the church and tries to help the man get up. He moans and collapses back to the ground. His leg looked strangely twisted so, our minister examines his ankle. He is surprised to hear a tiny voice speaking from the man's ankle saying,

"Please, can you lend me five dollars?"

Our minister ignores the voice and examines the man's knee. Again, he hears a small shrill voice that asks,

"Please, may I have five dollars?"

Our minister pretends the voice isn't there and touches the man's hip. The twisted hip responds with its own whisper,

"I beg of you. Please give me five dollars?"

Our minister is scratching his head just as the ambulance arrives. The emergency med techs ask our minister what is wrong with the man. He tells them,

"I'm not sure. But it sounds like his leg is broke in three places."

FAMILY

Our minister's mother was a seamstress.

His sister liked to darn socks.

His brother was a weaver.

His aunt liked to crochet.

He told us he came from a close-knit family.

PARALYSIS

Our minister was attending a large formal dinner. He was seated next to an attractive widow with whom he struck up a lively conversation.

Their talk wandered from spirituality, to economics and then to health issues. Our minister confided to the woman that he had remained healthy his entire life but still was consumed by irrational fears that he might someday become totally paralyzed.

The widow asked why he would think such an odd thing. Had he been paralyzed as a child?

"No." said our minister, "But I have a family history of age-onset paralysis. First my father, then my mother and just last year my poor older brother."

"How sad," replied the widow? "Perhaps..."

Before she could finish her statement, our minister jerked rigidly erect and proclaimed through clenched teeth.

"My God! It's happening.... I have total loss of feeling in my right leg."

The widow tried to calm the poor man down and whispered in his ear.

"It's all right Reverend. It is MY thigh that you have been pinching."

PATRIOTISM

Our minister had decided to honor all the members of our church who had died in wars defending their country. He had a huge plaque made with an American flag in its center and the names of those to be remembered listed below it. This plaque had been installed in a place of honor in the foyer of the church.

The following Sunday our minister stood in the entry and watched as church members filed in and stopped to admire to the fine new memorial.

Little Reggie came through with his family. The young boy looked at all the names and then approached our minister asking,

"Reverend, what is this new thing?"

Our minister gently explained that it was a special memorial to all the men and women who had died in the service.

To which Little Reggie replied,

"Which one? The nine o'clock or the ten-thirty?"

EMERGENCY!

A man came running into our church and grabbed our minister yelling,

"Come quickly Reverend! My wife is in the cab outside having our baby and there is no time to get to the hospital."

Our minister, who had been a medic in Vietnam, rolled up his sleeves, rushed outside and flung open the rear door of the cab. Inside a very large woman seemed to go into shock as our minister hiked up her dress and pulled down her panties.

Our minister felt a tug at his shoulder and turned to see the distraught husband pointing his finger toward the OTHER cab.

FRUGALITY

Our minister decided to save a few dollars on signs for our church. At the hardware store he purchased just four letters and placed all four of them on the front of the church door spelling 'OPEN'.

Then when he was locking the doors that evening, he moved the last letter to spell 'NOPE.'

SAYINGS

Our minister told us that if you don't have kindness in your heart, at least have the decency to be <u>VAGUE</u>.

Our minister said that there is GOOD in everybody. But I suspect he really hasn't met everybody.

Our minister said it is a blessing to say the right thing at the right time. And also to leave unsaid the wrong thing at a tempting moment.

Our minister said to be grateful for everything. So here I am staring in the mirror at the saggy wrinkles on my face. And being grateful.... that at least they don't hurt.

SLEEPING WITH MOM

Our minister returned home and his wife took him aside. She explained that during his absence, there had been a huge storm and that she had let their four children sleep in bed with her because they were frightened.

Our minister was appalled. His children were all older than six and the oldest was fourteen. So, our minister gathered his kids and told them that they were much too old to be sleeping with their mother and that in the future, if they were frightened, they merely had to turn to the 23rd psalm in their bibles.

Two months later, our minister was returning from a church retreat with several members of the congregation. His wife was to meet them all at the train station.

After a long wait, our minister spied his wife and kids in the crowd. Regrettably, his oldest boy got to him first and announced proudly and loudly that,

"We've got good news dad. No one slept with mom while you were away this time!"

THE MINISTER'S UNION

Our minister came home from church and told his wife that all of the ministers at the conference had just voted to join with a group of Jewish rabbis to form their own religious labor union.

"How wonderful," exclaimed his wife.

"Yes it is wonderful. But there were some drawbacks to the new benefits package we voted on."

"Oh, like what?"

"Well, we will be receiving long term health care insurance and a generous guaranteed severance allowance of $10,000.. "

"Wow, what's wrong with that?"

"Nothing, except for when you hear about what PART they will be SEVERING."

CAKE

Our minister went into a bakery. He asked the baker to prepare him a huge white cake forming the letters spelling out the name *'GOD'*.

The baker said that he could do this but that it would need to be done in many shaped pans and then the smaller cakes put together and iced. The entire project would take about three days.

Our minister agreed to wait and would return in three days. Three days later he returned and the baker triumphantly showed him the beautifully gilded white cake in the form of the letters 'GOD'.

"Ah," said our minister, it is beautiful, but there has been a slight misunderstanding. My order was for a cake in the form of an italic script *'GOD'*. And this cake is in the form of a block letter 'GOD'. I'm sorry, but it is not acceptable."

The crest-fallen baker looked sadly at his creation as our minister slowly dumped it into the garbage can. The baker recovered quickly and said that if the minister could wait three more days, he would prepare another cake exactly as ordered. Our minister agreed to wait three more days and then departed.

Three days later our minister returned to the bakers shop. On the counter stood a beautifully decorated white cake in the form of the italic script *'GOD'*.

Our minister inspected the cake carefully and then pronounced it acceptable "exactly as I ordered it."

The proud baker asked if the minister would like to take the cake with him or have it delivered to his house or church.

"Don't bother," said our minister. "I'll just take out my fork and eat it here."

GOLFING PRAYERS

I was playing golf the other day with our minister. Before every shot he would bow his head and say a little prayer before striking the ball. After the first nine holes I was behind by ten shots and having an awful day. So, I asked him during the turn if it might help my game if I said a few prayers? He surprised me by replying,

"Sorry, I don't think it will help."

"Why not?"

"Because you are such a lousy putter."

FACELIFT

Our minister was only in his sixties but many years in the sun as a boy had given him the hangdog wrinkles of a much older man. Not wanting to appear vain, he secretly went to an unlicensed surgeon while on vacation to get a face-lift.

The operation was a disaster and his tightened skin began burning almost immediately. By the next morning open infected wounds had appeared all over his face and he was taken to a hospital.

A plastic surgeon was forced to graft new skin onto his face after the infections were healed. Our minister returned home finally after a month's absence.

His wife admired his now-healed face and together they offered up a prayer of gratitude.

After the prayer his wife had to ask,

"Darling, where did they get the skin to repair all that damage?"

"I don't know," said our minister, "But every time I start to feel tired... My face wants to sit down."

CONFESSIONAL DEAL

A priest was called to attend to an emergency on a Saturday night in the middle of hearing confessions. Before leaving, he asked our minister to sit in for him for the rest of the confessions that night. Our minister said he did not know how to hear confessions but the priest assured him it was simple and he would show him the 'ropes' before leaving.

Our minister arrived and joined the priest in the confessional box. The priest tells him to just watch and listen for a while. A woman then enters the shaded confessional box and says,

"Forgive me Father for I have sinned."

The priest asks her to tell him,

"What is it you have done my child?"

"I committed adultery."

"How many times?"

"Three times."

"Well child, say three Hail Mary's, place a dollar in the donation box and sin no more."

The curtain opens, the woman leaves and another woman takes her place.

"Forgive me Father, for I have sinned."

"And your sin my child?"

"Adultery."

"How many times?"

"Three times."

"Well just say three Hail Mary's, put a dollar in the collection box and sin no more."

The woman exits and the priest tells our minister that he will be on his way. The priest leaves and the minister hears the curtain sliding open and the words,

"Forgive me Father, for I have sinned."

"And what are your sins?"

"Adultery."

"How many times?"

"Just once."

"Well you're in luck. You can still leave and come back later. We're offering a deal this week - three sins for a buck."

VANITY

A plump adolescent girl went in to see our minister after church.

"Reverend, I think I have committed the sin of vanity. Every morning I look into my mirror and tell myself how pretty I am."

Our minister peered out over his glasses before telling her.

" My child I have good news for you. What you have committed is <u>not</u> a sin. It is merely a <u>mistake</u>."

JESUS' IMAGE

The church janitor noticed one day that one of the church windows had cracked and formed the perfect image of Jesus with his arms outstretched. He bowed before the vision and then went to our minister's office with the news asking,

"What should we do Reverend?"

Our minister pondered a bit before answering,

"Look busy!"

THE FAITH HEALER

A famous evangelical faith healer was seated next to a minister on the train. The faith healer asked the minister how he was feeling. The minister relied that he was fine, but that he had a younger brother who was very sick.
The faith healer contradicted the minister saying,

"Your brother isn't sick. He only thinks he's sick. Let him know this and the power of his faith in God will make him well."

The minister thanked him for his advice and they parted at the next station.
Three months later, the faith healer recognized the same minister sitting alone as he boarded the train. He joined the minister and with a beaming smile asked,

"How is that brother of yours doing."

"Not so good," replied the minister. "Now he thinks he's dead."

PEEPHOLE

Our minister found a peephole carved into the wall of the church's bathroom.
A concerned woman in the church asked what he intended to do about it?
He replied that,

"He would be looking into it."

SAY IT WITH FLOWERS

Our minister goes into a flower shop to buy something for his wife on their first anniversary. The shopkeeper shows him a beautiful bouquet of roses for twenty dollars. Our minister asks to see something a little less expensive.

The shopkeeper shows the minister a colorful bouquet of mixed flowers for ten dollars. Our minister rejects the bouquet and asks the price of a single daisy.

The clerk replies the daisy will only cost one dollar. Our minister tells him he'll take the daisy and to please wrap it up. As the clerk is wrapping the lone flower, he asks the minister what it is he is trying to communicate to his wife with the gift?

The reply,

"I am a man of few words."

CHILI

In parts of Mexico the word chili is used as a euphemism for the male appendage. This is probably due to its phallic shape and its invigorating qualities in recipes. Our minister, Reverend Vainy who was in Mexico for the first time, knew none of this

Reverend Vainy was attending a worldwide Church conference and enjoying the local sights with one of the local Mexican ministers acting as his guide. After a quick tour of the cultural aspects of the city, Rev.Vainy invited the local minister back to his hotel for supper. Both men enjoyed a fine meal and decided to continue their conversation in the spa next door.

Each of the ministers had a mud bath and a massage and they were showering afterwards. Reverend Vainy finished first and stepped out into the dressing room to towel himself dry. Someone had left the dressing room window open and the cool night air caused him to shudder as he quickly pulled on his clothes. The Mexican minister stepped from the shower a few seconds later and as he was reaching for his towel, Rev.Vainy made the comment,

"Pretty chilly!"

His Mexican friend looked downward, his face a shade redder and murmured,

"Thank you."

TRULY NEEDY

After the Sunday worship service a young boy stopped on the way out of church to talk to our minister.

"When I grow up and have a job, I'm going to come by the church every week and give you all my money."

"Well thank you young man. And just what inspired you to think of such a generous act?"

"Because," said the earnest little boy, "my father said you were one of the poorest ministers we have ever had."

LUCKY NUMBER

Our minister had never gambled in his life. But the church desperately needed money for a new organ. The minister's lucky number had always been five. He had just turned fifty-five. It was May 5th. He decided to knell in prayer and read five pages from his bible. He blessed himself five times and headed for the racetrack.

At exactly five minutes after five o'clock he placed his entire savings of $555. on a horse named Cinco (Spanish for five) to win in the fifth race of the day. The horses were off! Our minister closed his eyes and said five prayers. The crowd was cheering as the horses raced to the finish line. Sure enough his horse had come in - FIFTH.

RICH FRIENDS

Our minister was wooing a very attractive blonde woman who attended services at his church. After their first year of dating he told her,

"I may not be as rich as some of my friends or live in a fancy house like some of my rich friends or be able to afford extravagant gifts like some of my rich friends, but I love you!"

"I love you too," she replied. " But, please tell me more about those rich friends."

FRUSTRATION

Our minister, a priest and a rabbi were having dinner together and got into a discussion about irritation, aggravation and frustration. What were the differences and which would be the most difficult to overcome?

The three decide a test is in order and our minister gets up to present his view of 'irritation'.
He goes to the nearby pay phone, places some coins in it, calls the town mayor and asks,

"Can I speak to James?"

A sleepy voice answers, "No, there is no one here named James," and hangs up.

"That," says our minister, "is an example of 'irritation'."

The priest gets up next. He goes to the same phone and calls the same mayor and asks,

"Is James there?"

The voice on the other end is a little more awake this time and it solidly responds,

"There is no James here." and hangs up.

"That." says the priest, "is a man who is aggravated."

The rabbi now gets up, puts his coins in the phone and announces to his friends, "now this is an example of 'frustration'." He calls the same number and asks,

"Hello, This is James. Do you have any messages for me?"

WORSHIP SONG

Our minister told the church organist that at the end of the service he would be asking for generous souls to stand up to donate toward the new church organ.

"That's wonderful", said the organist, "what song should I play for that?"

"How about, 'The Star Spangled Banner'?"

EXORCISM

A young farmer was having a problem with his wife's extreme moods. He began to think some evil spirits might possess her, so he called in our minister to perform an exorcism.

Our minister arrives the next day carrying a large black leather bag full of his exorcism equipment. They hear the wife moaning horribly upstairs and the minister tells the farmer to wait downstairs while he goes upstairs to conduct the exorcism.

Soon, the young farmer hears the minister grunting loudly in the upstairs bedroom. A few minutes later the minister comes down the stairs and asks the farmer for a screwdriver. The guy is puzzled but gets a screwdriver for the minister. The man takes it and goes back upstairs and there are soon sounds of more moaning and strained activity.

Our minister reappears on the stairway sweating and looking a bit worn out. This time the minister asks for a hammer and a chisel. The farmer gets them and the man disappears back up the stairs. There are more sounds of heavy grunting and some truly bloodcurdling shrieks. The young farmer is getting really worried and when the minister appears on the stairway again, he asks with pain-faced concern,

"Is... Is my wife going to be okay?"

Our minister takes a deep breath and looks back at the farmer before sputtering,

"I don't know. I still haven't gotten my *&*** bag open!"

COLLECTION BLESSING

Our minister had a monk from Sri Lanka speak to the congregation about his efforts in working with the needy people of his country after the great tsunami devastated its shoreline.

Our minister then explained that there would be two collections this Sunday. One for the poor and needy in Sri Lanka and a second for the needy in our own community. The collection bags for the needy in Sri Lanka came back full of donations. Rather than empty them, the minister passed around his own hat for the needy in the local community.

The hat came back completely empty. Not even a single coin! Our disappointed minister then had to bless all the offerings.

"Let us thank the Lord for all his blessings...and be grateful that my <u>hat</u> made it back AT ALL."

TITHING

Our minister decided to seek donations only from the wealthier church members because he realized that, not everyone is 'fit to be tithed'.

ANSWERED PRAYER

Our minister was in a conciliatory mood after delivering a heated sermon on the dangers of the new morality. As an example, he mentioned Brittany Spears, and how she should be more pitied than condemned. He suggested that his church members pray for her.
A young voice from the back of the choir was heard saying, "I've been praying for her for years. But I never get her."

ON THE PIANO

Reverend Ike has recently lost his wife of over forty years. Three spinster sisters from his congregation tried to lessen his burden by inviting him to their house for supper. After a wonderful meal, the women asked the reverend to join them in the parlor to sing some church hymns.
The reverend offered to provide the music and sat down at the seat in front of their lovely old piano. The sisters had gotten the piano from their bachelor brother who was now overseas. They didn't know how to play it and used it to store things.
Reverend Ike had to move several boxes and books from the top of the keyboard. As he did so, a large cardboard box fell from the top of the piano and crashed to the floor. When it hit the floor, the box split wide open and dozens of prophylactics spilled onto the hardwood floor.
The sisters saw the surprised look on the reverend's face and the eldest sister explained,

"Don't worry Reverend, no harm done. Those were just some of our brother's things. When he left we just stuck them on the piano because the box said they should be:

'PLACED ON ORGAN TO PREVENT DISEASE'

ITALIAN SONGBIRD

A visiting Italian minister was fond of singing in the shower. He didn't sing hymns but preferred the tunes from his boyhood. His rich voice could be heard emanating from the shower each morning as he sung,

"OH SOLO MIO."

God was not particularly pleased with this activity and decided to intervene. That night the minister had a stroke and half his brain was instantly paralyzed. The next day in the shower he tried to sing,

"O .. O..SO...SO...ME."

God didn't like this half-brained song any better and that night a second stroke paralyzed the rest of the minister's brain. The poor man didn't know what was happening. He didn't know where he was or what time it was or even who he was. Somehow he managed to pull himself out of bed and struggled to get into the shower. Here the warm water felt good and he felt his mouth relax as another song emerged,

"TIS IRISH EYES BE SMILIN."

DEAD ANIMAL

Our minister woke up early one morning and looked out his window at the church lawn. He saw what appeared to be a dead animal on the grass. The minister got up, got dressed and went to inspect the dead carcass. Sure enough, the dog-like animal had been dead for some time and was starting to smell.

Our minister went back inside and called the county Animal Control officer. He got Animal Control on the phone and explained that there was an ugly, stinking, dead, decaying animal on the church lawn and would they please come and remove it.

The Animal Control officer was a bit flippant with the minister and replied that,

"You're a church. Aren't you used to handling your own dead?"

Our irritated reverend responded that,

"Yes we do. But first we like to get in touch with the relatives."

BRANDY

It was well known that our church's minister was overly fond of apricot brandy. With that in mind, one of the church members sent the minister a case of apricot brandy as a Christmas present. In the next church bulletin there was a thank you in it that read,

'Reverend Guzzle would like to thank Brother Smares for his gift of fruit this Christmas Season and the spirit in which it was sent."

COUNSELING

Our minister was trying to help a woman with anxiety problems and asked her if she were having any unusual dreams.

"Why yes. One night I dreamed I was living as a squaw in a wigwam. The second night I was riding with Genghis Khan and sleeping in a yurt. What could they mean?"

"Maybe you are two tents?"

EMPTY CHURCH

Our minister looked out on an almost empty church before his Sunday service. He asked the head usher,

"Didn't they announce last week that I was giving the lesson this morning?"

The usher just shrugged and explained,

"No Reverend they sure didn't. But you must know how things like that leak out."

A DINNER PRAYER

Our minister asked little Billy in Sunday school if he had remembered to say a prayer each day before every meal.
Little Billy replied,

"No Reverend. We don't have to. My mother's a good cook."

ECUMENICAL

A priest and our minister were traveling together on the same plane. They were discussing some of the doctrinal differences between their two religions. The discussion became a little more heated when our minister stated,

"Its all right that we disagree. We are both doing God's work. You in your way, I in His way."

COJONES

Our minister was visiting Mexico for the first time. He was enjoying his stay and liked trying the different types of Mexican food at the hotel restaurant. This particular evening, he saw the restaurant special was something called 'cajones'. He asked his English-speaking waiter what they were?

" Ddees are de... how you say, testicles of ze bull. It is a long tradition to serve them after ze annual bullfight."

Our minister nodded that he understood and looked at the neighboring table where the patrons were enjoying plates of large globular meat in rich brown gravy. He ordered the "cajones' for himself.

The waiter returned with a piping hot dish containing globes in sauce but these were much smaller than his neighbors. He asked the waiter why his 'cajones' were so much smaller?

The waiter just held his hands out in reply,

"Ze bull. He not always lose."

BAND AIDES

Reverend Slosher was on his way home after imbibing a little too heavily. He turned a corner too quickly and fell off balance face-forward into a rose bush. The thorns cut deeply but he extricated himself and made it home. He entered quietly and stood in front of the bathroom mirror washing his cuts and putting band aides on the fresh wounds.

The next day his wife accused him of coming home drunk. Slosher denied that he had been drinking too much and wanted to know why his wife would make such a nasty allegation?

His wife took him by the hand and marched him into their bathroom. There she pointed to the mirror - it was covered with band aides!

INSANE CHOIR

Our minister was visiting an insane asylum in the state of Wyoming. It was the Christmas season and all the inmates were out in the hospital yard. Several of the men had on lovely velvet choir capes and were singing to their fellow inmates.

Our minister was impressed by the wonderful rhythm and the quality of the men's voices. Oddly, the singers each held a red apple that they struck with a long stick in time to the music.

Approaching the doctor in charge, our minister complimented the director for the quality of the music program. He even suggested that his church would love to host the singing inmates in the future.

"By the way," he asked, "what do you call this singing group, so that I can list them in our church bulletin?"

"Surely that's obvious," replied the director, "They're the 'Moron tap-an-apple Choir'."

DONATIONS

Our minister answers the phone one day.

"Hello, is this the 'Good Sheppard Church'?"

"Yes it is."

"I'm calling from the Internal Revenue Service. We were wondering if you could give us a little assistance?"

"I can."

"Wonderful! Do you know a Ryan Newby?"

"Yes I do."

"Is he a regular member of your church?"

"He is."

"Did he donate $20,000. to your church this year?"

"He will."

THE POOR

Our minister spoke to the Sunday congregation and reminded us that the church had made efforts to welcome new members from all socio-economic situations - and especially the poor.

And, holding up the nearly empty collection plate - announced sourly, "That they have come."

CAR TROUBLE

Our minister and his wife were sound asleep in their bed after midnight on a snowy winter morning when someone knocked loudly and persistently at the front door. Hoping they would go away, the minister pulled his pillow over his ears but the knocking continued until his wife finally begged him to go down and see whom it was.

At the front door was an unknown man. The man's hair was tussled as well as his clothing and the smell of alcohol wafted on his breath as he asked,

"G'Evenin sir. I hate to bother you but I was wonderin if you'd be good enuf to come out andgive me a little push?"

Our minister replied,

"Don't you know it's after midnight? And you are obviously drunk. Good night."

He shut the door loudly and returned to bed.

By the time the minister got back to his bed his conscience started bothering him. Muttering to himself, our minister got on his foul weather gear and grabbed the keys to his 4X4 truck with the tow bar and went back to find the drunk.

The drunken man was no longer at the front door. Our minister peered through the drifting snow and saw a dark shape under a tree in the front yard.

He called out,

"Are you there? I'm ready to give you that push."

An inebriated voice called back,

"I'm over here on the swing. It's about time. Wheeee!"

ELVIS

Reverend Joe spent twenty years serving our church. Now, after all that time, we had sent him to Las Vegas for a well-deserved vacation.

His plane ride to Las Vegas went flawlessly and he was reading the in flight magazine. There was so much to see and so little time. His pleasant reverie was interrupted as the flight attendant came by, looked at our minister and shouted,

" Oh my God! It's Elvis... You're not dead after all."

Reverend Joe looked around behind him and then to the sides. Then it dawned on him that the woman thought 'HE' was Elvis. He looked the young attendant straight in the eyes and admonished,

"Don't be a fool young lady. I can assure you I am not Elvis."

After this strange encounter, Reverend Joe made sure he was the first to de-plane and rushed to the baggage area. He got his suitcase and headed for the taxi stand outside.

As the cab driver came around to put his luggage in the trunk, the driver hesitated, looked at the minister and said,

"Oh my Gosh... Elvis. I knew you weren't dead. I've always been one of you biggest fans."

Reverend Joe wasted no time in telling the driver to,

"Stop all this foolishness. I'm not Elvis or anything like him. Now take me to my hotel."

Reverend Joe barely had time to stop fuming in the back of the cab before they arrived at the beautiful resort where he would be staying. Ignoring the still-staring cab driver, he got his own bag and entered the hotel lobby.

At the hotel desk the manager came up to him and loudly exclaimed,

"ELVIS! We knew the stories weren't true. We knew you'd be back some day. We kept your old suite ready for you - the one with the Jacuzzi; built in bar and an up-dated list of young show girl's numbers. Welcome back."

To which Reverend Joe scrunched up his face and replied,

"Thank you...Thank you very muchhh."

NEW CAR

Jimmy McNally had just won the first prize in the state lottery. He went to Rev Hooley after church that Sunday and told him that he had placed a $10,000. donation in the collection basket. Reverend Hooley thanked him profusely and told him that God would indeed be smiling on him and his family this day.

Then Jimmy said that he would also like to reward Rev. Hooley more personally for all his dedicated work to the church. He would give the Reverend the keys to a brand new Mercedes Benz convertible.

Reverend Hooley was stunned by Jimmy's generous offer but had to decline saying,

"Thank you Jimmy, but I know the church would frown on such an extravagant gift to one of its ministers."

"Well, in that case Rev., how about if I just sell you the car for fifty bucks? Then it won't be a gift."

Reverend Hooley stroked his chin in thought and then responded with,

"In that case Jimmy, I'd be happy to accept your offer! Here's $200.. I'll take FOUR.

DIET

Reverend Lardo was the heaviest minister our congregation had ever seen. His appetite was prodigious and it was not uncommon at a meal for Rev. Lardo to eat several chickens, a loaf of bread covered in butter, a pot of mashed potatoes and several ears of corn before asking for extra helpings of dessert and then washing it all down with a bottle of wine.

Our church board decided to visit the hefty minister at home and found him reclined in his favorite chair. Rev. Lardo's stomach protruded massively from his shirt. The head of the church board ordered that,

"Reverend Lardo! It is time for you to diet."

To which Reverend Lardo looked down at his stomach and replied,

"Shure nuff... What color would you like it?"

THE QUARTER

A new mother screamed for her husband,

"Help, our baby has swallowed a quarter off the floor. Should I call the doctor or call for an ambulance?"

Her husband told her to call our minister instead.

"But why our minister. Our baby isn't dying is he?"

"No. But our minister can get money out of anybody."

CHURCH PICNIC

Our minister arrived at the annual church picnic on a hot day dressed in a pair of shorts and a T-Shirt. A very pretty young woman who had recently joined the church and only seen our minister dressed in his Sunday suit remarked loudly,

"Gee Reverend, you sure look different with clothes on!"

ELDERLY MINISTERS

THE HEARING AID

Old Reverend Dishy was bragging to Reverend Bart about his new hearing aid.

"It's a marvel of modern technology. I can hear a pin drop, a leaf rustle or even the sound of hair being combed. This is the best hearing aid that has ever been invented!"

"What kind is it?"

"Oh, about ten minutes til five."

8 WARNING SIGNS THAT YOUR MINISTER IS GETTING OLDER

He keeps dropping his teeth on the bible.

His oxygen lines keep getting tangled.

He has a bathroom added behind the lectern.

He has fortunetellers offering to 'read' his face.

He sponsors and wins church 'belching' contests.

The snacks at church socials are now bran muffins and prune juice.

He likes to wear his old tie-died robes.

He sits in his rocking chair but can't get it going.

FISHING

Two retired ministers were out fishing together. They found a good spot in the shade of a riverbank and set up their fishing poles. For the next four hours they sat there motionless waiting for a nibble. Then one became a little restless and shifted to his side. The older minister barked at him,

"That's the <u>third</u> time you've moved your feet this past hour! Did you come out here to fish or to DANCE?"

JUDAS

There was an old Irish minister who had never gotten over the imposition of English rule in Northern Ireland. He used his Sunday sermons to rail against England and disparaged all Englishmen. The bishop received many complaints about this minister's fanaticism and finally ordered the minister to appear before him.

He told the old minister that he must not use his position to speak badly of the English and must learn to forgive them. From now on the bishop himself would select the topics for every Sunday sermon and the minister was not to stray from the assigned topic. The old minister grumbled but agreed to follow the bishop's orders.

The bishop assigned the minister a topic for the next Sunday. The minister was to speak about Jesus and the Last Supper. No other topics were to be mentioned. The old minister struggled to put together his talk. The bishop himself was in attendance that Sunday.

The minister began the service and then launched into his sermon. He quoted scripture about the role of Jesus at the Last Supper and was winding up his sermon with Jesus speaking to Judas.

"Judas, would thoust betray me?"

The old minister paused and fixed his audience with a baleful eye to convey the enormity of this betrayal as he had Judas reply,

"Not bloody likely, Guv."

THE BONE

An old Swedish minister had just finished wolfing down his entire meal. Suddenly, he looked up with concern and tugged at his wife saying,

"Becca, I, I tink I svallowed a bone."

"Are you choking Lemuel?"

"No, I'm therious!"

COMPLAINTS

The old minister went to the doctor's office and complained that he was having trouble reading aloud from his bible.

"And what do you think is the problem?"

"I'm pretty sure it's this," he replied pointing to his nose and what appeared to be an orange carrot growing out of his left nostril.

"My Goodness," exclaimed the doctor, "I've never seen this before. You must be pretty upset."

"You bet I am," stammered the angry old minister,
"I planted radishes!"

THE MASSAGE

An elderly minister retired to a small Florida town. He walks by a massage parlor every day and finally decides to go in to experience this thing called 'massage'.
A female masseuse sees the frail old minister come in and asks him to lie on the massage table. Out of curiosity she asks him how old he is.

"I'm 94 years old."

"Wheww!" says the masseuse, "you've just about had it."

"Oh, sorry," says the minister, "how much do I owe you."

GETTING OLDER

You know the minister is getting too old if,

1. Whenever he walks by a cemetery, the guys with the shovels start chasing after him.

2. When he goes to an antique auction, people start to bid on him.

3. His birth certificate is on a parchment scroll.

4. His blood type has been discontinued.

5. He just got a letter from a retirement home marked 'URGENT'.

6. His driver's license has a rating for wagons and buggies.

7. Pregnant women start offering him their seats on the bus.

8. He got slapped twice on his last date. Just to see if he was alive.

ANGEL WISHES

God's angels had taken notice of an elderly minister who had been especially devoted. They decided to reward the man while he was still in his body. Three angels were sent to appear at that Sunday's service and in front of the whole congregation offered the old minister his choice of any one of three earthly gifts.

The minister could have his choice of a million dollars, the good looks of a movie star or the IQ of a genius.

The old man thought for a moment and reflected that at his age, looks were no longer that important. As for money - he had always maintained a sense of prosperity about life in general. So, he would choose to be a genius.

The angels acknowledged his choice and disappeared in a flurry of wings.

The minister was left standing there with his head expanded with a new depth of wisdom and intelligence.

One of the church members stood up and asked the old minister what it felt like to now be so brilliant. And was there anything special he could now share with his congregation?

Looking around at his flock the old minister just shook his head and with his new wisdom replied,

"I SHOULD HAVE TAKEN THE MONEY!"

FALSE TEETH

An older minister was seated next to a layperson at a large ecumenical conference. He confided to the stranger,

"I am scheduled to be the next speaker but I left my false teeth behind in my hotel room."

The man smiled back and said,

"Reverend, God must be listening to your prayers because I happen to have an extra pair of false teeth in my briefcase."

In amazement and deep gratitude the minister took the proffered teeth from the man and inserted them in his mouth. They were too wide.

"Here said the man, I have another set that might fit you better."

The minister tried this set, but they were too small.

The man took a third set out of his case and assured the minister that this set would be the right one.

The minister inserted the teeth into his mouth and indeed, they were a perfect fit! Gratefully he shook the man's hand and praising God, he thanked his providence for being seated next to a dentist.

To which the stranger replied,

"No, not a dentist reverend. I'm an undertaker."

SPOONING

A very dapper well-mannered older minister asked a very modern woman who headed the church choir out on a date. Dinner together went well and in the car afterwards he leaned over and gently kissed the choir director's cheek and said,

"Back where I come from this is called 'spooning'. Do you like it?"

"Its okay," she relied holding him tighter and planting a big smooch on his lips, " but back where I come from, we prefer 'shoveling.'"

REMEMBERING NAMES

Our minister confided to a friend that he was starting to loss some of his memory. He was having a particular problem remembering the names of all his church members.

The friend advised our minister that he should just get around these awkward situations by asking them if they spell their name with an 'i' or an 'e'.

"That way they will usually spell their whole name out for you."

Our minister liked the idea and promised to try it out that very next Sunday after church.

Several weeks went by and the two friends met again. Our minister's friend asked him how the new method of remembering names was working?

"Well it worked pretty well at first. Then I had trouble with one of my favorite families when I asked if their name was spelled with the 'i' or the 'e'?"

"Really? What was their name?"

"Mr. & Mrs. Hill."

REVEREND HERB

A retired minister Reverend Herb had taken a part-time job as an air traffic controller. He was fired after his first week on the job after he got the following call from a pilot:

"Tower, I am unable to maintain altitude because my left engine has failed. I am low on fuel and my other engine is starting to flame out. What should I do? Please advise."

Reverend Herb was heard saying on the return transmission:

"To the pilot of Flight 230. Stay calm and repeat after me.
'Our Father who art in Heaven, hallowed be thy name....'"

ONLY IN AMERICA

Two elderly ministers were visiting California for the first time. They rented a car and visited Universal Studios and Disneyland. They enjoyed both parks and had time enough left to head to San Diego to see SeaWorld.

The ministers were on the road to San Diego when they stopped for gas in the pretty coastal town of La Jolla. They decided to get out and stretch their legs. There were a lot of tourists around and they heard the name of the town being pronounced in a variety of ways.

One asked the other,

"Do you think all of these pronunciations could be correct? La Joya, La Hoya, La Golla, or is there just one, most correct way to say it?"

The other minister didn't know, but thought they may be able to find out from someone who lived in town. So, they stopped at a restaurant and looked around for someone who looked like a local.

The obvious choice was an older man with white hair and glasses who was sitting there holding his dog. They approached this gentleman and politely asked,

"Sir, we are visiting from South Dakota. We are curious about your customs. Could you please tell us the correct pronunciation of this place?"

"Of course," said the kindly old man, "it is pronounced precisely the same as it is spelled,

T-A-C-O B-E-L-L."

PASSION

The congregation was surprised when they heard that their elderly minister had found 'passion' at the hospital.
They asked him about it when he returned,

"Was it with one of the nurses or with one of his visitors?"

The old minister was surprised at the question until he remembered his doctor's loud remark about his kidney stone,

"You're passing it! You're finally passing it."

A SIN

The old minister was sitting in the church resting after the Sunday service. He looked over as an attractive woman sat down in the seat next to him and spoke with a sense of charged urgency in her voice,

"Reverend, I think I may have sinned...I was going to work traveling just a little too fast on the freeway. All of a sudden this young highway patrol officer pulled me over. I tried to explain politely that I was sorry if I was going too fast, but that I had to get to work PRONTO.
Well this arrogant guy just interrupted and told me to shut up and hand him my license and registration. He smugly said he had me driving over the speed limit on his radar gun and I could beg and plead all I wanted but he was still going to give me a ticket.
I handed him my license and he looked at my picture and asked what kind of work I was in such a big rush for?

I told him, "I am a rectum stretcher."

That silenced him a bit before he asked, "A rectum stretcher? Just what does a rectum stretcher do?"

"Well." I explained, "first I get this small rectum on a conveyor belt. I insert one finger into it and then a second finger and then work them all-around until I can get my whole hand in. When I am done it is about six feet wide."

This got the cop to scratching his head and he asked, "And just what the Hell do you do with this six-foot rectum when you are done with it?"

To this I politely replied, "You give it a radar gun, a badge and park it on the freeway."

Now what I want to know Reverend ... was that a sin?"

SIN

An old minister was giving his last sermon before retirement.
A crying young woman came up to him afterwards and said,

"Reverend Bunnion, I am going to miss you so much. To think -I didn't even know what sin was until you came here."

NIGHTLY MIRACLES

An eighty-year-old minister went to see the doctor for his annual physical. He had been feeling a bit tired lately and wanted to know the reason. The doctor told him that everything seemed to be fine physically - all of his tests had come back normal.

"Perhaps," said the physician, "it isn't something physical. Are you sure everything is well with your relationship with God?"

"Oh yes," replied the old minister. "As a matter of fact I am so close to God that he even turns the light on for me when I get up at night and turns it back off when I return to bed."

"That's extraordinary," replied the doctor. "Well, just in case they might help, I'm giving you some vitamins to take. Maybe they will improve your energy."

The old minister left but his doctor couldn't get out of his mind the thought of the miraculous-light story. So, the next day on the way to his office, the doctor stopped by the old minister's house and asked to talk to his wife. The wife was much younger and seemed eager to find out if the doctor had discovered why her elderly husband was so tired all the time.

The doctor began to suspect it was the age difference but didn't say so. Instead he asked,

"Is it true that your husband and God are so close that God turns the light on and off for him at night?"

The wife's hand went to her mouth in horror. Shaking her head, she explained,

"That darn old fool. ... He's back to peeing in the refrigerator again!

GOSSIP

The old minister was attending a reception following the marriage of a friend's daughter. It was a marriage out of their faith and there were a lot of people present that were new to the minister.

As he went through the dinner buffet line, the minister noticed a woman on the other side of the line who was particularly unattractive. Not just overweight but poorly groomed, with large hairy facial warts, one over-sized eye and a stooped back.

Fascinated by the grotesque woman, the old minister nudged the arm of the man in line next to him and whispered confidentially,

"My God, that woman over there is so ugly she may be scaring the little children."

The stranger next to the minister stiffened and replied,

"I'll have you know that the woman there is my wife!"

The old minister was caught in his own gossip and now had to try to avoid an embarrassing situation so, he waved his hand to the side and said,

"No, no.... I meant that other younger woman next to your lovely wife."

"That woman sir... is my daughter!"

REPENTENCE

An unattractive young woman went into the church and told the minister,

"Reverend, I have been having problems resisting temptation. Last night I let the nice boy who had been elected prom king kiss me and then make passionate love to me six times."

The elderly minister winced and told the girl that she was to,

"Take six lemons, cut them in half and then squeeze the juice into your mouth."

"Will that keep me from sinning Reverend?"

"Maybe not. But at least they might take that smirk off your face."

35

AN HONEST MAN

The old minister couldn't find his favorite umbrella. He tried to remember where he had been the previous day and retraced his steps looking for the missing umbrella. After stopping at several places he finally arrived at the restaurant where he had eaten the night before. The waiter recognized the old minister and pulled the missing umbrella out from their lost and found box. The minister exclaimed,

"Finally an honest man!"

"What do you mean?"

"Everyone else in town denied having it!"

ALMONDS

A bus full of elderly female ministers is on its way to a church revival meeting. One of the ladies taped the bus driver on the shoulder and offered him a handful of almonds. The hungry driver gratefully takes them and munches on them as they continue down the highway.

A little later, the same lady taps the shoulder of the driver and offers him some more almonds. He takes them and this continues several times until they finally reach the large revival tents.

As the ministers gather their things to get off the bus, the curious driver asks the elderly minister why the ladies were so generous and why they didn't eat the almonds themselves - weren't they hungry?

The little lady minister smiled and explained that with their old teeth, they were unable to eat almonds.
The driver was even more puzzled and asked,

"If you can't eat the almonds, why do you buy them instead of something else?'

The sweet little old minister smiled again and replied,

"We just like to suck the chocolate off of them!"

HEARING AIDES

An elderly minister feared that his wife was losing her hearing. He went to their family doctor and asked what to do if she refused to come in for treatment?

The doctor explained that there was a simple test he could do at home with her to help her see that there was a problem. If there was then she might be more willing to come in for hearing aides.

He thanks the doctor and takes home the instructions for the hearing test. The next day he reads from the instructions and calls out to his wife from twenty feet away,

"Honey, What's for lunch?"

Hearing no response from the kitchen, he moves five feet closer and asks,

"Honey, can you hear me? What's for lunch?"

Still hearing nothing, he moves to within ten feet of his wife and can now see her as he yells,

"Honey, its lunch time. What are we having?"

When there is no reply, the minister steps closer, taps his wife on the shoulder and says,

"Honey I think you have a hearing problem. I've asked you three times already –What's for lunch?"

She turns to him and says,

"Jack, for the FOURTH time – its CHICKEN!

GETTING OLDER

Our minister is almost 85 years old and he doesn't need glasses.

"Wow!"

"Yeah, he still drinks right out of the bottle."

Our minister turned 85 and went to his doctor and asked,

"What can I do to make this wrinkled old face of mine look better?"

The doctor suggested,

"Take off your glasses."

Our minister's wife passed away at the age of 80. He grieved for a year and then went on the Internet and posted an ad seeking a young, sexy, Christian woman for an 85-year-old minister who needed romance in his life. He got only one response. It read:

"Try the nearest bookstore – under FICTION!"

THE MINISTER'S WIFE

LAST NIGHT

Reverend Dick was having some problems with an ache in his stomach. He finally decided to go to the doctor for an examination. The doctor touched the swollen stomach and ordered a battery of tests. The results came back later that day and he called Dick into his office.

"Reverend Dick, I have some bad news for you. You have a lethal cancer in your abdomen and it has gone too far for us to do anything about it."

Reverend Dick was shocked. His stomach was sore but other than that he felt fine. He asked,

"How much time do I have Doctor?"

"Only ten hours more ... at most. I'm sorry."

Reverend Dick stumbled out of the Doctor's office and headed home. He glanced down at his watch. It read five P.M. Only ten more hours! Reverend Dick started to run. His mind was a flurry of activity. He got home and wrote out a will. After that he called all of his friends and loved ones to say good-bye. He then got his wife and took her out to the fanciest restaurant in town and ordered everything on the menu.

When they got home from the restaurant it was after midnight. Reverend Dick kissed his wife lovingly and they proceeded to make love to her with an intensity neither of them had experienced since their courtship many years ago. They lay there exhausted in each other's arms as Reverend Dick said,

"Dear, that was wonderful. Shall we do it one more time?"

To which his wife replied,

"That's easy for you to ask. You don't have to get up in the morning."

OPTOMISTS SPEECH

A young minister was scheduled to give a talk to the local Optimist's Club on the subject of sex. When he got home after the talk he was reluctant to tell his wife that the men had been discussing sex so, when she asked about his talk, he said they had chatted about horseback riding.

The next day the wife is getting gas at a service station and was recognized by one of the men from the Optimist's Club. The man greeted her and complimented her on the fine talk her husband had given the night before.

She seemed a bit puzzled as she replied,

"Well, thank you very much. I am sure my husband will be very pleased. But I was a bit surprised at the subject matter he chose."

"Why is that?'

"Well, it is something he has only tried twice. The first time he got so sore he could hardly walk. And the only other time he nearly fell off."

SHOPPING

The minister took his new young wife to the shopping mall. He instructed her that they were only there to window shop and not to buy anything.

They met up a few hours later and the minister noticed his wife was wearing a brand new leather jacket. He admonished her with,

"I thought I told you not to buy anything!"

She responded,

"I didn't mean to buy it. But when I tried it on Satan appeared and told me how good it looked on me."

Her husband instructed her,

"You should have told him 'Get thee behind me Satan'.

She answered,

"I did. But then he got behind me and told me how good it looked from the back."

BAPTIST BRA

A minister sheepishly walks into the Lingerie department of a large store and asks the lady behind the counter for a 'Baptist' bra for his wife in size 38D.

The sales lady looks at him closely and makes him repeat his request.

"A Baptist bra for my wife - Size 38D Please?"

The sales woman looks at him appraisingly and replies,

"We don't get many requests for Baptist bras. I have helped people with Catholic, Presbyterian and Salvation Army bras though - are you sure you don't want one of those?'

"No," the man replied, "It has to be a Baptist bra. But what are those other bras like?"

"Well," explained the woman, "the Catholic bra 'supports the masses'. The Presbyterian bra keeps them 'staunch and upright.' The Salvation Army bra 'lifts the downfallen. But I have never heard of the Baptist bra. Does it do anything special?"

The little minister coughed nervously before explaining that the Baptist bra,

"Makes mountains out of molehills."

ABANDONED BABY

The minister's wife found a baby that had been abandoned in the church cornfield.

Together she and her husband raised the child and when the child got older he asked,

"Where did I come from?"

They truthfully answered,

"The stalk brought you."

MOOD RING

Our minister had grown up in the seventies and when he saw a mood ring at the flea market, he purchased it for his 'moody' wife. His wife was unimpressed with the gift but wore it anyway. The next day her friend asked her about the ring.

"My husband says it is called a 'mood ring'. "

"How does it work?"

" I don't really know. But when I am in a good mood it turns blue. And, when I am in a bad mood, it leaves a red mark on his forehead."

STAMPS

Our minister's wife went to the post office to get stamps for her Christmas cards.
The clerk asked her,

"What denominations?"

She thought for a moment before responding,

"Make that twenty Baptist, ten Catholic and a few Methodists.

LOTTERY WINNER

The stuffy old minister had married a much younger woman. She complained constantly about their poor finances. One day she arrived home unexpectedly, ran up the stairs to the parson's study and shouted at the top of her lungs,

" Reverend Jackson, pack your bags. I finally won the damn state lottery!"

The Reverend Jackson replies,

"That's wonderful Edith! But please don't use profanity. Anyway, What should I pack? My beach stuff or some of my mountain stuff?"

She replies,

"It don't matter. Just get the hell out!"

HEADACHE

The minister's wife had a headache and went to the pharmacist asking for 'oral-gesics'.

The pharmacist wanted to know why she wanted oral-gesics?

"Because the 'anal-gesics' had been too difficult to take.

THE MISTRESS

Reverend Scott Felden had been married to his wife for thirty years and to celebrate their anniversary, he took her to the theater. They were enjoying the play but during the intermission his wife found a long blonde hair on Scott's lapel. Both of them had dark hair. Rather than lie, Scott explained to his wife that he had been keeping a mistress for the past ten years. He then pointed out an attractive blonde woman sitting three rows in front of them and said,

"That's her."

The minister's wife started to cry. Reverend Felden dabbed at her tears with his handkerchief. He tried to make her feel better by explaining that mistresses were not that uncommon. As a matter of fact, he told his wife, the redhead sitting in front of them was Reverend Johnson's mistress.

The minister's wife looked curiously through her tears at the large redheaded woman seated in the next row. Her husband continued,

"And two rows to the left of us. Do you see that short brunette? She is Elder Hanson's mistress."

His wife looked at the frazzled little woman to which he pointed. She seemed to be coming to some conclusion as she stared at the women around her and said finally,

"You know what Scott? I think I like ours the best."

PLAYING CARDS

Our minister's wife loved to gamble. She had been persuaded to avoid casinos but still played cards with her lady friends each week. This particular night the ladies had gotten a little 'carried away' telling funny stories about their families. Before they knew it, it was after midnight. The minister's wife was feeling a little guilty about being out so late and tried to sneak in quietly when she got home.

She didn't want to disturb her early-rising husband so; she undressed downstairs, came up the stairs to their bedroom and slid naked into bed next to her husband. Our minister had not been completely asleep yet and sat up to turn on the light. He looked over at his nude wife and exclaimed,

"My God! Now you've finally done it. You've managed to lose everything."

CROSS ON THE LINE

A minister from Africa had recently arrived in America for the first time. He had never learned to read or write but knew his bible by memory. A banker helped the man set up a checking account for himself and his new church. Instead of signing his name, the minister would just annotate each check with two crosses (XX) as his signature.

This worked fine for several weeks until the banker started getting checks with three crosses (XXX) instead of two. The banker was unsure whether to pay the checks or not and went out to visit the African minister at his church. He found the minister alone and asked him about the three crosses instead of two?

"Oh yes," said the minister. "That be my wife's fault."

"Your wife's fault? How can that be? She isn't even on the account."

"Yes. But she's the one be thinkin that now we in America, I should be usin me middle name."

PROGNOSIS

The minister's wife took her husband to the doctor for his annual check-up. After an abnormally long wait, the doctor motioned the woman to join him in his office alone.

The worried wife asked if there was anything wrong. The doctor patiently explained that the minister was on the verge of a complete breakdown. And that the already frail man would surely die unless he got a warm healthy breakfast and at least one other nutritious meal every day. He would also need to avoid any stressful conversations or any taxing chores. The house would need to be kept scrupulously clean to avoid any contact with germs.

The wife thanked the doctor and returned to her husband in the waiting room. The frail minister asked his wife what the doctor had said?

Her reply,

"Sorry honey, he said you were going to die."

NEW WIFE

The minister was having problems with his new wife and the two could be heard arguing long into the night. One of his church members asked him the next day,

"Did you and your wife resolve your differences last night?"

"I'll say. She came crawling to me on her hand and knees this morning."

"She did? What did she say?"

Sheepishly, "Come out from under that bed you little coward!"

VISA CARD

Our minister told a friend that his wife had lost their Visa Card over six months ago.

"Have you reported it to your bank?'

"No."

"Why not?'

"Whoever found it is spending less than she does."

45

HOUSEKEEPER

The minister was approached by his wife while he was preparing his Sunday sermon. Stifling back her tears, she explained that their housekeeper had just given her notice and would be leaving at the end of the week.

This shouldn't have been a big deal but, this particular housekeeper was the best they had ever had, was hard working and the woman had become close friends with many of the members of the congregation including the minister's wife.

The concerned minister asked why 'Helga' was leaving with such short notice. The minister's wife explained that she had already asked Helga the same question. Helga had sadly related the story of having met and fallen in love with a racecar driver. The man was now gone but Helga was with child.

The minister and his wife prayed together about what should be done. The next day they called Helga into the living room and announced that Helga should continue to live with them and the minister and his wife would adopt the baby girl.

Helga stayed with the minister, his wife and the new baby girl but, the following year, the minister's wife again consulted her husband.
"Helga has decided to leave again. She has met some traveling basketball player, fallen in love and is with child again."

A bit more upset this time at the woman's easy virtues, but not wanting to have to raise the one-year-old baby alone, the minister called Helga in and told her they would adopt this child as well.

A lovely baby boy was born and joined the little girl as part of the family. All seemed well until the following year when the minister's distraught wife entered his study crying.
"Don't tell me," roared the minister, "Has Helga met a football player this time?"

"No," whimpered his wife, "she just left me a note that she has resigned."

"What!' exclaimed the minister, "After everything we have done for her. What was her reason?"

"She said she was leaving... because ... because, she hadn't signed on to work for such a large family."

46

ATTRACTIVE WIFE

The minister's attractive wife took her overworked husband in to see the doctor. The doctor took some tests and told his wife that,

"I don't like the way your husband looks."

She replied,

"I don't either. But he is good with the children."

BLIND MAN

A young minister's wife was alone at home on a Saturday afternoon. She decided to take a bath and had just finished disrobing when there was a knock at the front door.

"Who is it?'

"The blind man."

The young woman sees the man's dark glasses and gets a little thrill as she lets the man in while she is still standing there naked. As she searches for something to give the poor man, he asks.

"And where would you like me to hang your new blinds, M'am?"

SHAPELY

The minister's new younger wife was very proud of her figure. On their honeymoon she preened in front of the hotel room mirror and cupped her breasts with her hands as she showed them to her husband asking,

"What do you think of these? Cute? Perky?

The minister looked up distractedly, peered over his glasses, shook his head and replied,

"I just can't believe you took the time to name them!"

NEW CAR

The minister and his plump but pretty young wife were in the market for a new vehicle. He was looking at vans in the automobile showroom while his wife gravitated toward the convertible sports cars. All of the vehicles seemed awfully expensive to the minister. His young wife thought they should just put the purchase on their credit card and trust in the Lord. They decided not to make up their minds that day.

On the way home from the car lot, the young wife nuzzled up to the minister and whispered in his ear that her birthday would be coming up in another week. And if he would like to make it a perfect day for her, she would be delighted with anything that could go from zero to two hundred in less than five seconds.

The minister caught himself nodding in agreement and nothing more was said. A week went by and the minister's wife could barely control her excitement. The day of her birthday arrived and she looked out their window into the driveway. Nothing there!

She woke her sleepy husband and asked if he had remembered that today was a special day? He said he had and then wished her a happy birthday - and, by the way, there was a very special present waiting for her in the garage. Slapping her hands together in delight, the minister's wife flew down the stairs and pulled open the door to the garage. Inside sat their old Ford Taurus.

Hiding her disappointment, she noticed that in front of the old car on the floor was a beautifully wrapped package with her name on it. She kissed her husband and took the package inside. Her fingers tore at the ribbons and then at the box they contained. Inside the box was a gift that left her speechless in surprise - a brand new bathroom scale.

GREAT ORATOR

The minister had given an exceptionally profound Sunday sermon. It seemed to have gone a bit to his head as he bragged to his wife about it all week. Finally she had had enough when he asked,

"Do you know how few great orators there are in this country today?"

"No," replied his wife. "But I think its probably one less than you think."

THE FAIRY

An old minister and his wife were at a quiet little restaurant celebrating their 40th wedding anniversary. The waiter brought them a beautifully decorated cake at the end of their meal. Atop the cake was a candle in the shape of a forty. The loving couple held hands and decided to make an anniversary wish. Together, they blew out the candle.

As the candle flame died it was replaced by a tiny glittering fairy that hovered over the cake. With a tiny feminine voice the fairy spoke to them,

"For being such a loving and faithful couple all these years, I will grant you each one wish."

"Ohhh!" said the wife, "how lovely. I think I would like to wish for a larger house for our retirement. One with a whole house vacuum, a large but easy to care for kitchen and a large new study for my husband to write in."

With a twinkle of her nose and a smattering of fairy dust, the fairy said, "It is made so. And here is the deed to your new house."

Now it was the pragmatic old minister's turn. With some reflection he spoke,

"A new house is very nice. But this is an opportunity that only comes around once in a lifetime. Are you sure I can ask for whatever I want?'

The fairy's little girl voice assured him that this was indeed so.

"Well then," he said, "I'm sorry Dear, but my heart's desire is to have a beautiful wife at least thirty years younger than myself."

The wife and the fairy were very disappointed by his request. But, a wish is a wish... and with another smattering of fairy dust and a twitch of her nose... the minister's body began to shake, the wrinkles deepened and his body slumped as he aged instantly from 65 to 95.

Be careful what you wish for!

FAMILY WAY

The young minister and his wife had hired a Mexican girl named Carlotta to be their housekeeper. The girl seemed diligent and they were happy with the job she was doing. Then one day Carlotta came to the minister's wife and said she had to leave.

"But why Carlotta? Aren't you happy here?"

"Yes. But I am in the family way."

Taken aback, the minister's wife exclaimed,

"It can't be. Who is it? Who would do such a terrible thing?"

"Your husband and your oldest son."

"My husband........... And my son..." The minister's wife was crushed. How could these things have happened in her house? She gathered her courage and asked Carlotta to explain further.

"First I go into patio to clean, but your husband there and he say,

'Go. You are in my way.'

So then I go to living room to clean but your son there and he say,

'Go. You are in my way.'"

"So now I go because I am too much in family way."

SPENDING MONEY

One minister confided to a friend at the annual church retreat,

"I don't know what to do with this new young wife of mine. She's always asking for money. Twenty dollars last week, twenty again yesterday and just this morning she wanted fifty dollars!"

"My gosh," said his friend, "what does she do with all that money?"

The minister scratched his head before replying,

"I don't rightly know. I never give her any."

EGGS

A minister was getting dressed one day and happened upon a hidden bag behind his dresser. Inside he found three eggs and over a hundred dollars in currency. He called to his wife and asked her about his find.

The wife explained in embarrassment, that she had been secretly keeping the bag throughout their marriage. She had not wanted to hurt his feelings. But it had been her custom to place an intact egg in the bag every time her husband had delivered a poor sermon.

The minister reflected for a second and thought "Hmmmm! Three bad sermons in over twenty years. not bad!" Then he asked. "And what about all the cash?"

Her response. "Each time I got a dozen eggs, I sold them to the neighbors for a dollar."

ELDERLY WIFE

An elderly minister married one of his older female congregants and they left for their honeymoon. That night they undressed and slipped into bed together for the first time.

The elderly minister turned to his new wife and gently slipped his hand into hers and they fell asleep together. The next night he again held her hand and slipped into a peaceful sleep.

The third night the old minister moved to take his wife's hand again. She rebuffed him saying,

"Not tonight darling. I have a headache."

FRIENDLY

After the birth of their first child, our minister left the last church service to visit his wife in the hospital. Still in clerical garb, he greeted her with a huge hug and kiss. They whispered excitedly about the new baby and he gave her another huge kiss as he left. When he was gone the wife's roommate remarked,

"Gee-whiz, your minister is sure a whole lot friendlier than mine!"

LADY MINISTERS

HORSE RIDE

A lady minister had been born and raised in New York City. She had been given a new assignment to work at a church in West Texas. She welcomed the assignment, as she had always wanted to ride horses. But to avoid embarrassing herself when she arrived, she decided to get some riding practice in before she made the move to her new home in Texas.

Early one morning she got up and put on her riding britches and riding boots. She found the horse she wanted and managed to mount it without any problems. But, as soon as her bottom hit the saddle, the horse took off. It was a steady gait but it seemed to be picking up speed. She felt herself starting to slip from the saddle!

In desperation she threw her hands around the horse's mane and clung on tightly. But her right foot had slipped from its stirrup and her leg was hanging precariously and pulling her with it. She tried unsuccessfully to get the horse to stop. She could feel her hands slipping as well. Her face was now pushed hard against the side of the horse.

The horse's motion was battering her head along its flanks and she felt herself starting to lose consciousness. Then, she remembered a prayer from her childhood and silently called to Jesus for protection. As the words left her lips, she could feel the horse start to slow. Then the horse stopped and she was being lifted to safety by a set of strong arms.

Her prayer had been heard. It was Ralph! He was a member of her old congregation who worked at Wal-Mart. He had sensed her desperate prayer and arrived in the nick of time ... to UNPLUG HER HORSE.

THE SPA

The church's female minister was a wonderful orator but she was, how do you say it, 'physically unattractive'. The church members decided to chip-in and pay for her to visit a fancy beauty spa.

Afterwards they asked her husband if all the beauty creams and mudpacks had made her look any better?

He replied,

"Yes. But then, after a few days the mud began to fall off."

LOOKING FOR MISTER RIGHT

Two lady ministers who have been unmarried for some time decide to take a cruise together. Their first night on the cruise, the first minister Jane, notices an attractive-looking man seated by himself near the pool. She goes looking for her friend and says,

"LaMoura, I've just found this wonderful-looking man that looks lonely. You know how shy I am. Do you think you could go over and find out some more about him? Maybe he could even join us for supper?"

Her friend Lamoura agrees to find out more about the man and approaches his chair.

"Sir, I don't wish to intrude, but my friend and I are a little curious. You seem a little sad and we are both ministers. Is there anything we might be able to do to make you feel better?"

"You are correct. I am unhappy. But wouldn't you be a bit down too if you had just wasted the past twenty years of your life sitting in a dirty dank rotten prison cell?"

"I'm so sorry. I didn't know. What happened?"

"Well, if you really want to know... I accidentally stabbed my third wife with a kitchen knife. Thirty seven times."

"My goodness. That sounds so awful. You said third wife. What happened to your second wife?"

"No one is really sure. They found her head floating in the bay but her torso remains missing."

"And may I ask about your first wife?"

"We were very close. We were on a cruise ship just like this one. One night she fell off the side and was swept into the ship's propeller."

Lamoura could only shake her head. She didn't know what to say and wound up wandering back to her friend. Her friend Jane hadn't heard the conversation and asked,

"Tell me Lamoura, what did you find out?"

"Great news Jane. He's SINGLE!"

CLOCK SHOP

A very proper lady minister was visiting Israel for the first time. She was in the middle of her visit when she realized that her wristwatch had stopped working. Running late, She almost missed the bus with the rest of her tour group as it left for Jerusalem.

When they arrived in the Holy City, she went off to get her watch fixed. Walking down the busy streets alone and not able to read any of the signs, she was pleasantly surprised to find a little shop with several clocks in it's front window.

Entering the little shop, she approached a small-wizened man seated next to a desk.
"Excuse me sir, could you help me?" And she pointed at the frozen hands of her wristwatch.

"Yes Miss. I speak a little English. How can I help you?"

"Oh wonderful!" she exclaimed. "My watch is broken. Can you fix it for me?"

"I'm sorry miss. I don't fix watches. I am a moyl and I perform circumcisions on young boys and men.'

"But.... But if you don't fix watches.... why do you have all those clocks in your front window?"

"Miss. what would you suggest I put out there instead?"

REVEREND ALICE

Reverend Alice had been asked to be the keynote speaker at a large church conference. But, the night before she had developed an awful cold. She decided to say a prayer and attend anyway. The next day she felt a lot better and after taking two Tylenol, she stuffed two lace handkerchiefs in her bosom to take care of her runny nose.

Her speech was well received and she stayed for the dinner afterwards. Suddenly, just as she was seated between two of her most distinguished male colleagues, she felt a sneeze coming. She desperately reached into the left bosom of her dress for a handkerchief. Nothing there!

Doing her best to stifle the sneeze, Reverend Alice rummaged through the right bosom of her dress looking for a handkerchief. The sneeze escaped loudly across the table. Reverend Alice apologized, took her hands out of her bosom and explained to the shocked observers,

"I'm sure I had TWO of them when I got here."

MILK BATH

Our minister's doctor advised her to bath in milk three times a week. So, the next day the woman requested that the milkman deliver eighty gallons of milk to the church. The milkman asked her,

"Do you want that pasteurized?"

"No," she replied, "just up to my chin."

RELIGIOUS WRITER

Reverend Mary Kate decided to spend her free time away from her duties at church by writing fictionalized accounts of Jesus and his life with the apostles. She submitted her first story to the Bob Jones University newspaper for publication. It was returned with a rejection form letter.

Reverend Mary Kate puzzled over the reason for her rejection and after much prayer decided that it must have been her use of the words 'mad as heck' to express Jesus' dissatisfaction. So, she replaced the words with 'stern disapproval' and resubmitted her story with a note reading,

"I have cut the 'heck' out of my article and hope you can now see fit to publish it."

Her manuscript came back four weeks later with the following response attached,

"Dear Reverend Mary Kate. Without trying to appear irreverent, you can cut the HELL out of this story and it still wouldn't work."

WINDY DAY

It was a very windy day in a little English coastal town. A female minister was coming out of church hanging onto her cap. A sudden powerful gust blew her long dress up into the air and around her ears.

The embarrassed minister was just pulling it back down when a local man walked by and said,

"Its pretty airy today isn't it?"

The minister haughtily replied,

"What did you expect ... FEATHERS?"

VISITING ITALY

A group of women ministers from the U.S. was visiting Italy for the first time. At a museum a docent was assigned to lead them on a tour of the great art and architectural wonders. He watched as the women gathered around each masterpiece with reverence and awe.

One of the American women seemed to be particularly impressed with the works of the old masters. She beckoned the docent over to her near the end of the tour and pointed at a lovely old oil painting by Botticelli and asked to know more about the artist.

The docent began to explain how Botticelli had lived in Florence.

"No. Not Botticelli," interrupted the lady, "I want to know about the artist called 'Circa'.

The docent wasn't sure what the woman was talking about so he asked,

"Are you sure you mean 'Circa'? I don't know any artists by that name."

The woman minister continued,

"Oh, I'm sure you do. He's the most prolific artist we've seen today. Look, here's another one of his works."

There on the tag below the painting was the inscription, 'Circa 1665'. And right next to it another painting by 'Circa 1882', and another "Circa 1778'.

LIBERATION

Two older female ministers at a church conference were talking to each other about the restrictions they had faced growing up as women. They decided to celebrate their new freedom by taking off all their clothes and 'streaking' through the hotel lobby.

Two older male ministers looked up as the women went racing by. One said to the other,

"My word! What kind of outfits were those two ladies wearing?"

The other replied,

"I don't know. But whatever they were, they sure needed ironing."

THE HAIRDRESSER

A newly ordained woman minister had just been chosen to lead the congregation in the small community of Leeds, England. This church had a long history of male-ministers-only and the choice of a woman had upset some of the older, more traditional members.

One of these happened to be the town hairdresser. The new minister had heard these rumors and decided that she would seek the woman out and have her hair done before she left to visit London.

The minister found the hairdresser's salon and introduced herself while complimenting the woman on her dress and the lovely decor in her shop.

Despite the compliments, the hairdresser's dour expression never changed. She seemed almost displeased when the minister asked if she would style her hair. The quiet in the shop felt overwhelming as the hairdresser grudgingly motioned the minister to sit in the salon chair and began to cut her hair. Finally, the hairdresser asked out of curiosity, why the minister needed her hair styled - wasn't her old cut good enough?

The minister explained that there was nothing wrong with her old style but that she was making a special trip to London this week and wanted to look her best.

The hairdresser wrinkled up her nose and said,

"London? Why would anyone want to go there? It's crowded and dirty and cold and foggy. You have to be crazy to go to London! So, how are you getting there?"

"Oh, I'm flying on Brit Air and I got such a great rate that I'll be using the savings to donate to our church Sunday school."

The hairdresser ignored the generosity and replied,

"Brit Air! That's a terrible airline. The planes are old and cramped, the flight attendants are ugly and they always arrive late. So, where are you staying in London?"

"I found a lovely inexpensive place near the British Museum called the Jenkins.'

"Ha," replied the hairdresser, "I know the place. My friend thought it would be nice too. But it's old, smelly and really a dump - probably the worse hotel in the city. So, whatcha going to London for anyway?"

"I'd like to visit Westminster Cathedral and maybe see the Queen."

"Yeah, right.... you and a million other people. You'll be lucky if she's even in town this week. You'd better be prepared for a really rotten week. You'd be better off not going."

The minister didn't know how to respond, so, she just thanked the woman politely, left a generous tip and left to begin packing.

A month later the minister was back in town and had begun her ministry. The hairdresser was noticeably absent from the Sunday services. Rumor was that the woman's pride and obstinateness would keep her from ever attending while a woman was in the pulpit.

The minister decided to visit the woman again at her salon. Taking a seat to get her hair done, she could see the hairdresser snickering to her other customers and pointing at the minister in derision.

When it was the minister's turn, the hairdresser asked loudly enough for the other customers to hear,

"So, how was your trip to London?"

"Oh, it was wonderful! My flight was overbooked, so they moved me to a first class seat next to a handsome and spiritually interested businessman. The food on the flight was wonderful and my hotel had just finished adding a brand new suite that they let me use for the same price."

The hairdresser wrinkled up her nose and smugly muttered,

"That might be all well and good. But I bet you didn't get to see the Queen."

"Well, the Queen wasn't around when I first walked by Buckingham Palace. But a uniformed guard tapped me on the shoulder as I was going by and pointed to a tiny gate. I entered the gate and the Queen herself was standing there. She was handing out special greetings and I was able to walk right up to her, get one, and even talk to her a bit."

"Reallllyyy...And what did she have to say?"

The minister smiled to herself for a brief second before answering a little more loudly,

"She said, 'where did you get that crappy hairdo?'"

ATTACKED

An unattached lady minister was taking a Caribbean cruise vacation. Suddenly, as the woman was walking the deck, she was attacked by a deranged African crewman who threw her to the deck and raped her.

The ordeal finally ended and the crewman was taken away in chains. After three weeks of waking screaming in the dark, her friends told her she had to pull herself together, find forgiveness in her heart and get on with her life.

"But.... she painfully explained. "He hasn't written. He hasn't even called!"

GUESSING HIS AGE

An older woman minister is sitting outside her retirement center in Florida. An elderly man comes along and asks the woman if she would be kind enough to guess his age? She agrees to guess. But first she tells him that he must take off all of his clothing, including his hat and shoes.

The old man seems a bit perplexed by this request but starts stripping off all of his clothes. After removing his hat he is standing there covered with nothing but his wrinkles. He asks again,

"Guess how old I am today?"

"Not so fast. First you need to bend over as far as you can and shake like a dog."

The poor man is starting to feel a little humiliated, but he does as the minister requests. When he is done shaking he is a bit light headed but asks,

"Guess how old I am today?"

"Not so fast. Just one more test. You must stand on one foot, flap your arms and whistle."

The old man has no dignity left but he does as the woman asks. He hides his exposed privates with one hand and asks,

"Please lady, tell me how old you think I am today?"

The lady minister considers carefully all she has just seen and replies confidently,

"You are exactly eighty-four years five months and three days old today."

The old man is shocked. The guess is precisely correct! He asks the minister how she could be so sure of his age? Was it one of the tests or was she just psychic?

She explained patiently,

"No, I'm not psychic. You are just one day older than you were when you were here yesterday."

TRAIN CONDUCTOR

A group of lady ministers are taking a train ride back from a religious conference. The train conductor comes by and asks the women for their tickets. They show their tickets. All except for Bernice, who can't seem to find her ticket. She fumbles in her purse. She looks in the crease in her seat. She fumbles some more in her purse.

Meanwhile, the train conductor is doing a slow burn. The man has had a bad day and the train is running late. He tells the lady to hurry it up. Rev. Bernice ignores the conductor and continues to fiddle in her purse. The man is enraged.

When Bernice starts to look in the crease of her seat one more time, the conductor can't take it and slaps her across the face. The train authorities take the conductor away, he is tried and convicted of assault and battery and on the way to prison, he kills one of the guards.

Now the conductor is convicted of murder and sentenced to die in the electric chair. He is about to die when he is asked if he has any last requests. He says he would like to have Reverend Bernice forgive him and say a prayer for him. Reverend Bernice arrives and says a prayer. The switch is thrown and electricity shoots through the conductor's body. His body starts to smoke a little but he doesn't die.

There is a standing law that a reprieve is given whenever a miracle like this happens and the conductor is allowed to go free. He thanks Rev. Bernice and heads back to the railroad company he used to work for. They will not give him his job back. The conductor gets angry and a fight breaks out. He punches another employee and accidentally kills the man.

The conductor is convicted again in court and because of his prior crime is sentenced to die. He is again given one last request and again asks for Reverend Bernice to come and say a final prayer for him. The switch on the electric chair is thrown and after the sparks stop flying the conductor is still sitting there unharmed.

The warden is amazed and disturbed that he will again have to free this killer. The warden turns to Bernice and asks about the power of her special prayer for this man. She replies that,

"Warden, I don't think so much that it's the prayer.

I think this man is just a bad conductor."

REMEMBER ME

An older female minister left the church early in the morning for her first visit with a new dentist in town. When she arrived, the dentist's waiting room was almost full. She took a seat and waited for her turn. On the wall above her head were the dentist's school diplomas and credentials. She saw his full name printed there and remembered back almost forty years.

There had been a young man by that same name in her grade school class at St. Joseph's Church. The young man in her memory had been very intelligent and handsome. His curly blond hair, blue eyes and beatific smile had left a favorable impression in her memory. Could this be the same man?

Then, there he was in the hallway calling the next patient into his office. This man didn't fit her memory. He was almost bald with thick glasses, massive wrinkles on his face and he walked with a stoop. But there was something about him ... could he really be her old classmate?

When her turn finally arrived, the minister was ushered into the dentist's office by his assistant. There in his chair she had a good view of the man. And there was something very familiar about him so, she asked,

"Excuse me? Did you ever attend Bible College back in the forties?"

"Why yes. Why do you ask?"

"I think you were in my class in 1948."

The dentist scrutinized her face a little more closely. Despite the passage of time she felt her heart doing a pitter-pat and she smiled up at him before he replied,

"Maybe, what subject did you teach?"

COFFIN

Two lady ministers are walking home together late at night. It is dark and the wind is picking up as they pass a graveyard.

"I think I hear something."

"No," says her friend, "its only the wind."

"No. I definitely hear...."

And now they both could hear it. A definite,

"CLUMP...CLUMP...CLUMP..."

"What is it?"

"I don't know but I think we'd better start walking faster!"

The two women start walking as fast as they can. The sound behind them increases in intensity,

"CLUMP...CLUMP...CLUMP..."

Behind him they can just see a coffin-like box pursuing them in the dark. The ministers both start to run.

"CLUMP...CLUMP...CLUMP..."

The ladies reach the door of their hotel and race inside slamming the door behind them. But the coffin can be seen through the keyhole. It is now throwing itself against the door trying to get in!

"CLUMP...CLUMP...CLUMP..."

A third lady minister comes out of her room and sees her two terrified friends. She reaches into her pocket and hands them each a Smith Brothers lozenge. The women take the lozenges but inquire,

"How will these help, Rev. Lucy?"

"I have it on good faith that these will help stop the coffin."

SPELLING

A female minister was visiting India. At a small restaurant in Calcutta she found herself seated next to a table where three Indian yogis were having a heated discussion in English. Without being rude she tried to listen to them. The first yogi was saying,

"You must spell it the simplest way 'w-o-o-m-m'."

"No," said the second, "I believe it is 'w-o-o-m-b'."

The third replied insistently that the correct spelling would be 'w-o-o-o-m-b-r'.

Our lady minister had heard enough. In her best attempt to be helpful and demonstrating Christian kindness, she got up and approached the men at the table saying authoritatively,

"The correct spelling is 'w-o-m-b'." And then she graciously excused herself and went back to her own table.

The three yogis looked astonished as they watched her leave. Then the first yogi said to the other two,

"Do you suppose she is right?"

"I don't know," said the second.

The third replied that he thought the lady was just a little too young to know how to spell the sound of an elephant fart.

MISSING TOE

A lady minister is driving down a lonely country road on her way back to her church. She hears a siren and an ambulance races by her with its lights flashing. The ambulance hits a bump, an ice chest falls out the back but the ambulance keeps going. The minister stops her car and picks up the ice chest. Inside she finds a frozen toe.

The minister picks up her cell phone and calls the hospital. They thank her for calling and ask her to wait there until they can send someone back to pick up the toe. She agrees to wait and is sitting there in her car waiting when her cell phone rings. It's her husband wanting to know what is taking her so long to get back? She thinks and then answers,

"I'm okay. I'm just sitting here on the side of the road waiting for a TOE TRUCK."

DATING A MINISTER

Two single women ministers were meeting for lunch. The first was a blonde named Rev. Mary who asked her brunette friend Rev. Rachel about a young man who happened to attend church in both their congregations.

"Rachel, I understand that you went out with Sam Mauler last month. He has asked me out too, and I wanted to talk to you first before I give him an answer."

"Well Mary, He did show up for our date on time. He is a handsome man and was impeccably dressed. He brought me a beautiful bouquet of flowers and held the door of his new convertible open for me.
We went to dinner at an expensive new restaurant, had a fabulous meal and went to a great play afterwards. He's a wonderful conversationalist with a witty sense of humor. I'd never had so much fun on a date.
But, when we got back to my house, he tried to kiss me good night on my porch. When I resisted, he turned into an animal and began pawing at me and ripped my new dress.
I finally had to push him away and slam the door."

"My Goodness Rachel, what a story. I guess I'm going to have to turn down that date."

"No Mary, don't do that. I'm just suggesting that maybe you shouldn't wear a new dress."

MAKEOVER

An overweight female minister named Reverend Mabel had a massive heart attack in the middle of her Sunday sermon and was rushed to the nearest hospital. She received an immediate operation but remained in a coma for eight days before regaining consciousness.

While in the coma she had a near death experience and while moving through a tunnel of white light, met a radiant being that she knew was Jesus Christ. Jesus told her that her mission on Earth was not complete and that she must return but that they would meet again in forty years.

The minister cried as she related this story to the doctor at her bedside and wondered aloud what things she would need to do with her remaining forty years. The doctor assured her that her heart now appeared completely healed. He then suggested that while she was in the hospital she have a nose job, liposuction and a complete makeover so that she would look good no matter what she was supposed to do.

The minister agreed and ten days later looked into a mirror at her new thin self. Her hair was now two shades lighter and beautifully coifed. Her new slim nose matched her now thinner body. She felt ready to go out and do God's work.

She chatted happily to the cab driver as he drove her back to her home near the church. But as she got out of the cab and crossed the street, a teenager in a truck slammed into her and she was instantly killed.

She found herself back in the tunnel of white light. Ahead of her she saw Jesus. Upon reaching His side, she looked into his radiant eyes and inquired why He had not rescued her from the truck?

Jesus looked back at her closely.

"Mabel, is that you? I didn't even recognize you."

65

SUNDAY SCHOOL

MORALITY LESSON

A church elder decided that a visual demonstration would add a dramatic emphasis to that Sunday's church lesson. In front of his Sunday School class he took out a jar full of dirt. From the dirt he extracted four long wiggling earthworms.

The first of these worms he placed into a jar of alcohol. The second he placed in a jar filled with cigarette smoke. The third wound up in a jar of pure sugar. And the last worm was placed in a jar containing fresh organic vegetables.

The elder placed the four jars under his desk and continued with his lesson. At the end of the class he had the students watch as he retrieved the four jars. In the first jar with alcohol the worm was dead. In the second jar with cigarette smoke the worm was dead. In the third jar with the sugar the worm was dead. But in the fourth jar the worm was thriving amongst the fresh vegetables. He asked the class what this demonstration meant to them?

Little Billy had his hand up first.

"Yes Billy, what did you learn today?"

"I learned that.... if you drink alcohol, smoke and eat a lot of candy.... you won't have worms."

MEMORIAL DAY

The Sunday School teacher was telling the young children in her class that Memorial Day was a celebration of the great country we lived in and the brave men who had fought to defend our rights to all be 'free'. A young boy stood up in the front row raised his hand and stated,

"But I'm not free. I'm <u>four</u>."

VISITORS

Little Billy was attending the Sunday church service with his parents. After the service he told his mother that he needed to ask the minister something about his sermon. His mother was pleased that he had been paying attention and took Billy to the minister's office.

"Reverend," asked Little Billy, "I heard you say in the sermon that our bodies come from ashes and dust?"

"Yes, that is correct Billy."

"And that when we die our bodies go back to being dust?"

"That's correct, 'Ashes to ashes and dust to dust.'. But why are you so concerned about it Billy?"

"Well Reverend, I think you need to come over to our house right now."

"Why is that Billy?"

"Well I think you need to say a prayer or something under our furniture. Because there's a whole bunch of dead folks hanging out there."

SPELLING

The Sunday School teacher asked the students in her class to raise their hands and tell the class where they had spent their summer vacation. A little girl in front waved her hand and stood to tell the class that her family had gone to the beach. It had been a lot of fun and she had made a bunch of new friends there.

The teacher thanked her for sharing and told her if she could spell 'water' she would receive a candy bar as a reward.

She spelled "W-A-T-E-R" and received her candy.

A tall boy in back raised his hand, stood and told the class that his family had also gone to the beach. He had made new friends as well and they had built sand castles together.

The teacher thanked him for sharing and asked him to spell 'sand'.

He spelled "S-A-N-D" and sat down with his candy bar.

Oscar, who was a little Puerto Rican boy, raised his hand. He stood to tell the class that his family was also at the beach. But because of his dark skin color, no one would play with him all summer.

The teacher looked at the small boy and told him that he still could have a chance to win a candy bar. He just first needed to spell 'prejudice' for the class.

MANNERS

A Sunday School teacher and some of his students were in the men's rest room at the same time. One little boy finished his business, zipped his pants and headed for the door.

"Wait a minute young man," called the teacher, "didn't your parents ever teach you to wash your hands after peeing?"

"No, Sir. They taught me that it was a lot better not to pee on my hands."

SUNDAY SCHOOL OUTING

The church Sunday School had been planning an outing for the third-graders end of the year party. The local racetrack offered to let the children visit during the day for free. They could have their picnic there, pat the horses and learn about horse care at the same time. Two third grade mothers agreed to come along to provide extra supervision.

The kids were very excited and after the picnic several needed to go to the bathroom. One of the mothers was assigned to take the little boys to the bathroom and the other mother was to take the little girls.

The first mother was standing outside the men's room waiting for the boys when one of the little ones appeared and told her that the urinals were too high up for him to use. Having no other choice, she looked inside the men's room to make sure there were no men present, and then seeing none, stepped inside.

She put her hands under the youngster's arms and lifted the boy up to the men's urinal. But her arms were pinning the boy's arms up in the air and he couldn't reach his zipper. She set him back down and helped him lower his pants. Then when she hoisted him up, she was able to reach around and direct his pee-pee away from his clothes with her hand.

The mother repeated this process with two more small boys but as she raised the next boy to the urinal, she noticed the little boy was unusually well endowed. As he finished and she was lowering him back down she stated,

"Aren't you a big boy? You must be almost ready for the fourth grade."

"No Mum," he replied, "I'm the jockey in the fifth race riding Golden Cloud."

WHISTLING

A stern Sunday School teacher, told a young boy to stop whistling while he was reading his assignment. She heard him whistling again a few minutes later and whacked his hand with her ruler and took him to see the minister.

The minister asked the boy why he had been whistling while he was reading?

The boy protested,

"No. That's not true Reverend."

"Are you calling Mrs. Hagly a liar?"

"No Reverend. She's not lying. She is only wrong."

"What do you mean ... wrong?"

"Well, I was whistling ... but I sure wasn't reading."

GOD'S PICTURE

A Sunday school teacher was having her young students work on art projects for display at the church's annual Christmas celebration. One boy was drawing a reindeer. Another a Santa Claus. A third a Christmas tree.

But then she got to Reggie, who had been a bit of a problem in the past. His hand was busy making swirls of color across his paper. The curious teacher asked what he was drawing?

Reggie replied,

" I'm drawing God."

"Oh!" replied the teacher. "But Reggie, no one knows what God looks like."

Reggie, undaunted and not even bothering to look up from his drawing responded.

"They will in a minute, Teach!"

STRETCHING A POINT

A Sunday School teacher found some gum under one of the seats and holding it up, asked her class,

"What is the stretchiest substance on Earth?"

Little Billy raised his hand and she called on him.

"Teacher, the stretchiest thing on Earth is human skin."

The teacher was surprised by the answer and responded with,

"I don't think so Billy. Human skin is very pliable but do you think it is as stretchy as this piece of gum?"

"Yes teacher. And it even says so in the Bible."

The teacher tried to remember her Bible stories but nothing came to mind so, she asked,

"Billy, could you please tell all of us where in the Bible does it speak of human skin being stretchy?"

"Yes teacher. It was in the part where Jesus tied his ass to a tree and walked the rest of the way into Jerusalem."

NATIVITY PICTURES

The Sunday School class was listening to Christmas carols and after hearing a moving version of 'Silent Night', they were all asked to draw a picture of the baby Jesus in the nativity scene. The teacher walked around admiring the children's wonderful renditions of that first Christmas.

Then she noticed something odd in a picture Little Billy had drawn. There was a strange obese man in a cloak hovering over the baby Jesus. She asked Little Billy about it. He cheerfully explained that,

"Oh, that's Round John Virgin."

GOD'S SON'S NAME

The Sunday School teacher asked young Billy if he knew the name of God's son. She was shocked when he answered,

"Andy."

"Why would you think that God's son would be named 'Andy'?"

"Because of the song."

"What song is that?"

"You know teacher. The one that goes,

'Andy walks with me, Andy talks with me
Andy tells me I am his own."

THE CADILLAC

The Sunday school teacher asked her students to draw a picture of their favorite story from the bible. At the end of the hour the children handed in their drawings. The teacher commented on each one, praising each child for either the wonderful blue color of Jonah & the Whale or the realistic figures in Jesus' feeding of the multitudes in the 'loaves and the fishes'.

Little Sammy was the last in line to turn in his picture. The teacher hoped to find something positive to say to Sammy because he had been struggling to keep up with the other kids in the class. But, as she looked at his picture she was speechless.

In Sammy's picture two very naked people were rolling around in the backseat of a large car driven by a bearded hippie. Flipping the picture to hide it from the other children, she tried to contain her upset as she asked.

"Sammy. What is this?"

"Gee teacher," replied Sammy, "it's a Cadillac."

"No Sammy. I mean what bible story is this supposed to represent?'

"Don't you remember teacher? It's just like you said - its God driving Adam and Eve out of Heaven."

JESUS' FATHER

The minister asked his young Sunday School class whether anyone knew the name of Jesus' mother?
One bright five year old replied,

"Mary."

"That's correct," said the minister. " Now can anyone tell me the name of Jesus' father?"

A little boy in back put his hand up and yelled,

"It's Verge."

The minister was a bit confused by the boy's response and asked why he thought Jesus' father would be known by that name?
The little boy said that it was in their bible stories.
The minister wanted to know which one?
The boy answered,

"The ones where they are always talking about 'the Verge and Mary'".

HEARD IN SUNDAY SCHOOL

"Did Noah have a wife?"
"Yes. She was named Joan of <u>Ark</u>."

"Why was Jesus' mother called the Virgin Mary?"
"Because she had an immaculate <u>contraption</u>."

"What is St. Paul remembered for?"
"He's the one who <u>cavorted</u> to Christianity and preached Holy <u>Acrimony</u>."

"Were Jesus' teachings accepted by the Jewish people while he was alive?"
"No, he had some problems with unsympathetic <u>genitals</u>."

"Which is your favorite Commandment?"
"Though shalt not <u>admit</u> adultery."

"Can we hear some more stories about Jesus and his twelve recycles?"

GRAFFETI

A new addition to the church school was being built. The senior minister looked out his window to observe the project. Shocked, he sees several of the Sunday school children pressing their hands and names into the newly poured concrete.

Dashing out of his office, he screams loudly and shakes his fist at the offenders as they dashed away.

One of the ladies of the congregation witnessed the outburst and admonished the minister,

"Reverend, aren't men of God supposed to love little children?"

To which he agitatedly replied,

"Yes, in the abstract. But not in the concrete."

COUNTING THE COMMANDMENTS

The Sunday School teacher had just finished her lesson about the ten commandments. She then asked her kindergarten class if any of them could actually count out loud the number of commandments handed down by God? Little Lucy raised her hand and started counting out loud,

"One. Two. Three. Four. Five. . Six. Seven. Eight. Nine and Ten."

"Very good Lucy. And if God had given us even more commandments ... what would those numbers be?"

Little Lucy looked down sadly and said she didn't know.

Little Billy raised his hand excitedly. When no one else looked up, the teacher asked Little Billy to continue. He shouted proudly,

"Jack. Queen and King!"

Ten Signs that you need a new Sunday School Teacher

1. "Teacher, teacher, are you sure this is how they made unleavened bread in the bible?"

   - "SHHHH! Just get back in the oven with the other children."

2. "Teacher, teacher, Billy says I look like a Baboon!"

   -"SHHHH! Just be quiet, comb your face & get back in line."

3. "Teacher, teacher, I keep trying to run, But I only go in circles!"

   -"SHHHH! Be quiet or I'll nail your other foot to the floor."

4."Teacher, teacher, jimmy won't let go of my ear!"

   - "SHHHH! Jimmy please let go of Lizzy's ear.
     Jimmy, Let go of her ear! Ohh! Okay Jimmy, put that
     ear down right here & get back to your seat."

5. "Teacher, teacher, why are you pushing the church bus into the lake?"

   - "SHHHH! You'll wake all the other kids."

6. "Teacher, teacher, my head hurts."

   - "SHHHH! Just be quiet and hold that dart board a little higher."

7. "Teacher, teacher, can I go out to recess now?"

   - "SHHHH! Just light my cigarette and deal the cards."

8. "Teacher, teacher, Jimmy says my head is too big."

   -"SHHHH! Just move your hat out of the bathroom so we can use t."

9. "Teacher, teacher, is it time for lunch yet?"

   - "SHHHH! Just leave the dead squirrels in the bag & be quiet."

10. "Teacher, teacher, I don't think I like swimming."

   - "SHHHH! I'll tell you when to get out of that sack."

NAUGHTY

Our minister asked the Sunday School class if they knew,

"Where do little boys and girls go if they are naughty?"

Little Reggie piped up first,

"TO THE BARN HAYLOFT?"

THANKSGIVING

The Sunday School teacher brought in a Thanksgiving Day card showing a Pilgrim family on its way to church together. He held it up to his class as an example and said,

"See how happy this early Christian family was to go to church together."

One of the students put up his hand and asked,

"Then why is the dad in the picture walking behind them with a gun?"

PARENTAL MODELS

"Dad, did you go to Sunday School every Sunday when you were a boy?"

""Yes son. I went every Sunday even if I was sick or didn't want to go."

"Yeah, I thought so. I don't think it will do me any good either."

MINISTERIAL STUDENTS

GREAT SALESMAN

A young ministerial student was unemployed and needed money to continue his studies. He went looking for a part-time job. He saw an advertisement in the local paper for a sales agent for 'The Good Book'. The young man called to make an appointment to apply for the job. When he arrived he found a small office stacked with bibles. The owner was there and asked the man if he had ever sold bibles before. The young student replied,

"Nnnnooooo. I-I-I hhhaaaaveeee nev-nev-neverrrrr d-d-donneee th-th-thattt."

The owner of the store looked at the student and asked him,

"It might be very difficult for you to sell these with your nervous speech problems. Are you sure you want the job?"

"Y-Y-Yeessss. I-I-I nnneeeeddd th-th-the m-money."

"Okay. I'll give you a chance. But remember that I warned you that it might be difficult for you. And if you don't make any sales by the end of the week, I'll have to let you go."

The student thanked the man and took a box of bibles with him. The week went by and the student returned to the office. The owner was there and was a bit shocked as the student placed a stack of ten-dollar bills on his desk. He had sold the entire box of bibles. This was more sales than anyone else in the office. The owner had to ask,

"Congratulations! You've done a great job this week. But I am curious. What is it that you say to the people when they answer the door?"

"I-I-I jjjusssttt sssay t-to th-th-them. D-d-do yyou wwwwant tto b-b-buy a B-B-Bible?
Oooor d-d-do you w-w-want m-m-meee t-t-to j-j-justtt r-r-readdd it t-t-to y-y-you?"

TELLING A JOKE

A new student had recently arrived at the Bible College and was preparing for bed in his tiny dormitory room. As he pulled his one blanket up to his chin, he heard the number 'eight' shouted loudly down the corridor followed by uproarious laughter from the other student's rooms.

Three more numbers were shouted out and each was followed by bellowing laughs and guffaws.

The new student was curious and got up and visited the guy in the room next door.

"Brother, what are those numbers I hear being called out?"

His fellow student explained that the men in this dormitory had been together so long that they had memorized each other's jokes and instead of re-telling the whole thing each time, they just shouted out the number of some of their favorites.

The young student thanked his new friend for the information and went back to his room. While lying there listening to more numbers being shouted and the laughter that ensued, he decided it might be fun to join in. At the next pause between 'jokes', he yelled out,

"FOUR!"

There was a deathly silence. So, he tried again.

"SIX!"

Again, there was no response. So, he decided to use a number that had previously brought a gleeful response and yelled out,

"EIGHT!"

There was no response at all and the joke telling seemed to be done for the evening. The new student went to sleep perplexed by his failure to illicit any laughs from the other guys in the dorm. The next day he went next door again and asked the student there,

"Brother, why is it that no one would laugh at the numbers of the 'jokes' I called out last night?"

The other student thought carefully for a second and then answered,

"I guess some guys just don't know how to tell a joke."

THE BEAR

A ministerial student saw his friend washing dishes in the group kitchen. Usually this was a chore reserved for those that were being punished. His friend was one of the nicest men he knew. What could he have done to warrant this kind of treatment? He decided to ask,

"Lucas, why are you stuck with the dishes?'

Lucas looked at his friend with a beatific smile on his face and explained,

"I was doing my walking meditation out in the woods. I stopped to hug a tree and a huge bear started growling at me. I smiled at the bear but this just seemed to make it madder. I turned to leave and it started chasing me. I just managed to get back to the dormitory and slam the gate with the bear right behind me."

"Wow! That's quite a story. But you should be rewarded for your getaway. Why are you being punished?"

"The Dean heard that I had been running around with a bear behind."

YALE

The minister was interviewing several of the ministerial students as candidates for a new youth ministry. One man was particularly impressive. Good looking, young, well groomed and with an air of competence. He would make a perfect example for the church's youth. The minister then asked if the man had any education beyond high school and the answer was,

"Yale".

"Wonderful," said the minister, "a fine school. I have some good friends who've attended there. And, by the way, what is your name again young man?"

"Yackson."

WOODEN LEG

A ministerial student arrives at a Bible College out in the country and is assigned to work with the animals on the school's farm. He is surprised to see a pig with a wooden leg kneeling in prayer next to the barn. That evening he asks the head of the school about the unusual pig.

"Yes, that is Hector, the pig. He is a very special pig, blessed with a huge heart, a special intelligence and a spiritual intensity. He is much loved by all of us here at the College."

"I've never heard of a pig that prays before."

"Hector not only prays but he loves the bible so much that we have given him his own copy that he keeps in his pen. He truly seems to understand its message of service to others. When we had a big barn fire two years ago, he raced through the fire to rescue the other animals. He is a very, very special little pig."

"Wow, that is pretty special. And how did he get his wooden leg?"

"Well, with a special pig like Hector ... you don't want to eat him all at once."

BLIND SKYDIVER

A blind young ministerial student wanted to do something different and decided to try skydiving. He had a friend take him out to the airport where he was directed to the manager of the local skydiving team. The manager looked up as the blind ministerial student walked into his office. The student was wearing dark glasses, one hand held his long white-tipped cane and the other a leash holding his seeing-eye dog. The manager asked,

"Can I help you?"

"I want to sky dive."

"Aren't you blind?"

"Yes."

"How will you know when to pull the rip cord?"

"When the leash goes slack?"

THE QUIZ

Two young ministers, fresh from seminary school, were both interested in the same newly open position at a large city ministry. The church board looked closely at the qualifications of the two young men and found them closely matched in almost every way.

Both were asked to deliver a Sunday sermon and both did so eloquently. Afterwards, the church members were surveyed and it was obvious that the congregation was evenly split between the two men.

The senior member of the church board was asked to prepare a quiz to test the candidate's bible knowledge. The winning candidate would be chosen from their answers to this all-important quiz.

The church elder took his task seriously and prepared ten questions arranged in an increasing order of difficulty. He would also be grading the quiz and delivering the results to the board.

The test began with both candidates writing furiously and with great intensity. When the allotted time ran out the church elder collected both exams. An hour later he returned the graded exams to each man. As might be expected, they had both answered nine of the ten questions correctly.

That night the church board called the men back in and awarded the ministerial position to the first of the two men with condolences to the second.

The second candidate was filled with indignation and demanded an explanation from the board.

Quietly, the church elder, who had prepared the quiz, took the young man aside. He explained that the appointment had been made not on the answers that had been given, but rather based on the one incorrect answer. The man still did not understand until the elder held the two answers up for him to compare.

The winning candidate had written,

"I don't know" to the final question.

The loser had written,

"Neither do I".

GUIDELINES FOR STUDENTS VISITING New York City

1. The city does not employ 'wallet inspectors'.

2. It's considered bad manners to lie down in someone else's chalk outline.

3. If you see something that looks like chili but doesn't smell like chili - it isn't chili.

4. Cab drivers frown on 'blessings' as tips.

PAINTING THE PORCH

Elmo was a mute ministerial student who needed to make some extra money for his Bible College tuition. He found an ad in the local paper that read,

'Help wanted at Sven's. Must be able to paint.'

The next day Elmo went into town to apply for the job at Sven's Nursery. Sven was a big hulking man and he looked down warily at the small ministerial student. After a quick appraisal, Sven handed Elmo the paintbrushes and a gallon of paint.

"Here," he said, "take these and paint the porch in back of the house. Come see me when you're finished!"

A few hours later, the little student was back at Sven's front door. Sven was a bit surprised at how quickly the young man had worked.

"Finished all ready? Did you do a good job?"

Elmo scribbled out a quick note in response. It read:

'Yes, and I even had paint left over, so I gave it a second coat.'

Duly impressed, Sven reached into his thick wallet and pulled out a hundred dollar bill and handed it to the little man.

The Dean of Students was waiting for all the students that evening and ushered Elmo into his office upon his return. Elmo handed the Dean the hundred-dollar bill and with a happy smile left to join the other students at supper.

The Dean looked at the hundred dollars in his hands and was about to put it away with the other school funds when he heard a loud pounding at his back door. The secretary had gone home, so the Dean answered it himself.

Sven stood at the door towering over the Dean with a look of red-faced rage covering his face. The Dean invited the angry man in and asked what was the matter.

Sven ripped a piece of paper out of his pocket and threw it down in front of the Dean saying only that he had found it attached to his car's windshield wiper. The Dean put on his reading glasses and immediately recognized Elmo's handwriting,

'Thanks for the job. But it's not a Porch, it's a Mercedes."

THREE-LEGGED CHICKENS

A ministerial student has just arrived at a small country church. Out in the churchyard he passes a small pig, a donkey and a three-legged chicken. He has never seen a three-legged chicken before so he stops to look at it for a while. The senior minister comes along and sees the young man staring at the chicken.

"Young man. What are you doing?"

"I'm sorry Reverend. Its just that I have never seen a three-legged chicken before."

"Well, it is a bit unusual, but we have raised an entire flock of three-legged chickens here through selective breeding techniques."

"But why three-legged chickens? Why not something else?"

"There is a reason behind the three-legged chicken. At our evening service we usually serve chicken. But all of the members prefer dark meat and request chicken legs. There just weren't enough to go around so, we decided that with three-legged chickens, everyone could have a leg if they wanted."

"That makes a lot of sense. Do they taste the same as a regular two-legged chicken?"

"I don't know," replied the Reverend shaking his head, "we still haven't managed to catch one."

BLOOD DRIVE

The dour bible college president was rarely seen out of his office. But this day he called a general meeting and was exhorting all the ministerial students present to become more involved in the community, to work to improve the image of the church, to make a difference!

Then he proclaimed the coming month as 'WE GIVE' February. The school would open its doors to the community and the first function would be a community blood drive.

The old leader proclaimed that he would lead the way by donating the first pint of blood.

To which a dubious student in back replied,

"I wonder whose?"

ETHICS CLASS

A young man was taking a class in ethics at the bible school. The instructor asked him what he would do if he saw two trains approaching each other on the same train track - would he say a prayer, go for help or try to throw the switch lever himself?

The young man replied that he would try to throw the switch himself.

"Fine," said the instructor, "but what would you do if the lever was jammed shut?"

The young man said he would take his shirt off and wave it to warn the on-coming trains.

"Fine," replied the instructor, "but what if it was dusk and the train engineers wouldn't be able to see you?"

"In that case, I would send for my minister."

"Your minister? And what could he do?"

"Nothing. But he just loves to watch train wrecks."

CLUES THAT YOU MIGHT HAVE A MINISTERIAL CALLING

1. You always catch yourself counting all the attendees at sporting events.

2. You always jiggle all the toilet handles at church before leaving.

3. People fall asleep when you are talking.

4. You feel guilty when fishing or golfing on Sundays.

5. Your friends get 'Pissed off" but you feel 'Grieved in the Spirit'.

MISSIONARIES

JUNGLE TRAP

Two Christian missionaries had lived amongst the native peoples in the jungles of Africa for over two years. A very crafty man-eating lion had killed and eaten three of the villagers and the natives were in fear for their lives. The best hunters in the village had been unable to catch the sneaky beast.

The two missionaries offered to help out and got the villagers to dig a deep pit to trap the lion. They baited the trap with raw meat but the lion didn't take the bait. Instead it went into the village and ate another native. It seemed this lion truly preferred human meat.

The missionaries realized they couldn't use a real human or even a dead one to bait their trap so they decided to do the next best thing. One of the missionaries was an artist and he drew a very lifelike representation of a sleeping villager. He then placed it at the top of the hay-covered pit after rubbing the picture with the smell of fresh meat.

The next day the two missionaries raced out to see if their trap had been sprung. At first sight they realized that they were dealing with an abnormally bright lion. The trap was still sitting there unsprung. But not only that, there was evidence that the lion had seen and understood what they were up to. Because ... the picture of the native was now gone and in its place was ...a <u>picture</u> of the lion!

NATIVE CLUB

A missionary had just arrived in darkest Africa. He was alone and on his way through the jungle looking for a certain tribe when he encountered a native pygmy. The tiny pigmy warrior was holding his short little spear over the head of an enormous lion that lay dead at his feet. The lion's head alone was much larger than the little black man. The surprised missionary asked in the native language of the area,

"Did you kill this huge beast?"

"Yes. Kill lion with club and spear."

"Wow! That's a pretty tiny spear. You must have a very powerful club."

"Yes. Very powerful. Almost fifty members."

STUCK

A missionary was captured by a fierce tribe of cannibals. They tied him to a tree and each day would stick a knife into him only far enough to make him bleed and then all the cannibals would drink his blood. This went on for a month until the missionary finally asked the cannibal chief,

"Please, please give me the knife so I may kill myself."

"Is it not a sin for a Christian to take his own life?"

"Yes, but I'm tired of getting stuck for all the drinks."

JIMMY

Jimmy the missionary was a bit of a problem for the church leadership. In civilian life Jimmy had worked at a muffler shop but he left it to join the church because he found it was too 'exhausting'.

The church leaders had tried to find a spot for him in the church's soup kitchen but he couldn't cut the mustard. When asked to add spices to the soup, he said he didn't have enough thyme to do it right. He also didn't like making the morning coffee saying, it was always the same old grind.

He was finally asked to leave the kitchen entirely when his orange juice came out too watery because he couldn't concentrate.

Putting him in charge of the youth ministry's pool didn't work either because he found it too 'draining'. He tried leading their morning exercises but he wasn't 'fit' for the job.

As a last resort, Jimmy was given the church's donated clothing and asked to mend any holes he found. Jimmy quit at the end of the day because he thought it was only a sew-sew job and he wasn't really 'suited' for it.

The last we heard, Jimmy had gone back to school to become a doctor. Things were slow at his new office because he didn't have enough 'patience'.

AUSTRALIA

A missionary was visiting Australia for the first time. As he crossed the road, a motor scooter struck him from behind and knocked him unconscious. When he woke up in the hospital in pain and wrapped in bandages he tremblingly asked the nurse,

"Was, Was ... I brought in here to die?"

"No," said the nurse, "you were brought in here yesterdye."

KEEPING THE COMMANDMENTS

A missionary was sent by his church to bring God to the natives in darkest Africa. He arrived and began living with a local tribe and preached to them daily from the Bible with special emphasis on keeping the Ten Commandments. Part of his daily refrain was 'Thou must not covet thy neighbors wife or possessions. Thou must not fornicate or commit adultery outside of marriage'.

The missionary was soon considered an honorary member of the tribe. Then one day a village leader approached the chief of the tribe and whispered that his daughter had just given birth to a child - and it was WHITE.

The chief was shocked and sent for the missionary. The young missionary arrived and took a seat across from the chief. The chief wasted no time in explaining the purpose of this visit.

"Brother Joseph, we have welcomed you into our tribe and allowed you to preach your white man's wisdom. But now a white child has been born and you are the only white man in this region. What say you to me about your preaching about the sin of fornication?"

The young missionary was in obvious discomfort but knew he was not guilty. He looked the chief square in the eye and tried to explain how the birth might be genetically possible by citing this example,

"Chief, I think you are mistaken. You and your tribe keep sheep here in the village for wool and meat. Now most of the sheep are white - but doesn't there occasionally occur the presence of a black sheep?"

The chief looked back at the missionary with a comprehending nod of his head and replied,

"Okay Brother Joseph, I understand better now. If you won't say anything about the sheep, I'll be quiet about the white child."

AFRICA

Two young missionaries had been captured by a wild uncivilized African tribe of cannibals. The men were tightly bound, stripped naked and placed in a huge pot of water.

As all seemed hopeless and the fire beneath the pot grew warmer, the first commented optimistically to his half-cooked friend...

"At least they'll get a taste of religion!"

ANSWERED PRAYER

A young Christian missionary is walking across the Indian subcontinent. He is crossing a set of railroad tracks and his foot slips and gets caught between the rails. He struggles to get loose, loses his sandal but remains firmly stuck. In back of him the tracks start to rumble with the sound of an approaching train. The desperate missionary begins to pray,

"God, I beseech thee, please rescue my foot from these tracks and I will remember you with my every thought."

Nothing happens and the foot remains stuck. The missionary prays even more deeply,

"Oh God, I will surrender up to you even the tiniest of my meager belongings, my favorite tea set and even my worldly friends, but please rescue me!"

The train is getting very close now and suddenly his foot flies out from between the tracks and he leaps to safety just as the train rumbles past. The missionary gets up shakily, dusts himself off and retrieves his missing sandal. He looks up to Heaven and says,

"Thanks anyway God, but it looks like I got out of this one by myself."

TERRORISTS

A missionary schoolteacher in South America was captured by terrorists and told that he would have to have sex with one of his teenage female students or the terrorists would burn down the church. The new church had just been completed so the teacher reluctantly agreed to have sex to spare the church - but - only under three conditions.

What were these 'conditions' - the terrorists wanted to know.

"First," said the teacher, "whichever girl you pick must be blindfolded so that she doesn't see this terrible thing being done to her."

"Second, she must be given ear plugs so she can't hear what is being done to her."

"Agreed," said the head terrorist. "And what is the third condition?"

"She must have large breasts."

SPREADING THE GOOD NEWS

A young missionary had searched for a missing tribe of headhunters in the jungles of New Guinea. He finally found the tribe and took out his Bible to begin spreading the good news of the Lord. He took the chief of the tribe aside, opened the book to scripture and explained,

"The good book says that even though you have lived as God-less heathens.. you may still be saved."

The old grizzled chief replied, "Uhh Guntay."

"It says that if you stop eating your brethren, you will find Jesus."

The chief looked him in the eyes and replied, "Uhh Guntay."

"It says that if you keep the Lord's Day holy and learn to love your enemies you will be shown the kingdom of Heaven."

Once more the chief replied, "Uhh Guntay."

The young missionary was very pleased at this first evangelical session. He thanked the chief for listening and was on his way to the hut he had been given when one of the villagers stopped him abruptly. The native's brusque hand on his shoulder hurt as he pulled away and he grimaced a bit as he looked to see what the native wanted.

The native couldn't speak English, but tried to explain with gestures his reason for accosting the missionary. The native pointed down at the trail. The missionary had been about to step into a stinking pile of fresh animal dung. The native pointed at the pile and shook his head, held his nose and explained aloud,

"Uhh Guntay."

CANNIBALS

Two cannibals were sitting around the fire complaining about their lives. The first cannibal says to the second,

"I hate my mother-in-law."

The second replies,

"So try the potatoes."

PASSION

An earnest young missionary was trying to give a pretty young girl a ride home. She was not a practicing Christian and seemed to have had a few too many alcoholic drinks.

The young man tried to keep his composure but the young lady kept leaning over and breathing into his ear saying,

"You're passionate!"

He pushed her away and told her,

"I know you've had too much to drink. I like you too, but this isn't the right time for romance. I know you live around here somewhere. Is it the next turn?'

To which she replied,

"No. That's what I've been trying to tell you. You're passin' it."

NICE TAN

A returning missionary was visiting a beachside community and was invited to a welcoming party down by the ocean. He had not been out in the sun for many years and his skin was very pale. To avoid getting a sunburn, he went to the drugstore and asked for a strong suntan lotion.

The clerk offered him a tube of spf 14 cream and explained that it offered all day protection for most people. The missionary looked at the tube and asked if there was anything stronger.

The clerk rummaged on his shelf and produced a tube of spf 32 cream. the missionary looked at this tube very carefully and asked,

"Is this the strongest sun protection you have?"

The clerk went into the back of the store and returned with a large tube marked spf 100 and said,

"This is the strongest sun screen we carry. It is guaranteed to prevent any burning."

The happy missionary thanked the clerk, paid for the spf 100 tube and headed for the beach party. In the bathhouse changing room the missionary removed his clothes and opened his new sunscreen product. There was some surprise on his face as the tube was opened and.....
a jacket fell out!

CHINA

A newly arrived missionary was greeted by a large Chinese delegation dressed in their finest clothing. The missionary realized that a wedding ceremony had just been performed in Chinese and that he was to now give a Christian blessing on the new couple.

He was searching for the right words as he was invited to a podium in front of the group. There he was asked by one of the group to please explain 'elections'.

This seemed an odd question but the young missionary went with it and gave a lengthy explanation of the democratic process. The crowd lost interest after a few minutes and began disbursing.

One young couple was heard whispering as they wandered away that,

"What dat got to do wid Chinese blide-glooms?"

GOT RELIGION

A young missionary was living with the Inuit (Eskimo) people in northern Alaska. he was doing his best to fit in with their different life-style. So, as the Eskimo hunters were leaving for an overnight hunting expedition in a distant forest, he asked if he could join them as an observer.

They agreed to let him come and dressing warmly he joined the group as it left for the forest. Later in the day the missionary walked away from the group to answer nature's call. He returned to find the group had left without him. Panicking, the young man called out for his companions.

The hollow echo of his own voice filled him with dread as he noticed the sky starting to darken a bit. Then, in the dusk, he saw a bulky figure approaching. Rushing toward the form, he stopped in his tracks. It was a mammoth brown bear!

Turning on his heels, the young missionary ran for his life. But no matter how hard he ran, the bear kept getting closer. Finally, exhausted and unable to continue, the missionary threw himself to his knees and pressing his palms together skyward, implored his Heavenly father to,

"Convert this wild animal's beastly appetites and give it some religion."

The sky darkened further as the bear came to an abrupt halt in front of the young man. Lighting flashed around them and the great beast looked confused. Then with it's paws extended skyward, the bear spoke,

"Thank you God... For that which I am about to receive."

HOT DOGS

The young missionary returned from Africa with a young African convert. His family welcomed the young man and invited him to stay for dinner. The missionary's mother asked her missionary-son what she should prepare that evening?
He replied,

"Oh, anything distinctly American. Our African brother is very interested in our food and culture."

That night they all sat down to eat. On the table was a bowl of hot dogs with all the extras. The young African man looked distraught and asked to be excused from the table without eating anything.
The concerned mother asked if he didn't like hot dogs?
The African replied remorsefully that,

"In Africa we eat dog too. But not THAT part!

THE SHAMAN

A missionary to a remote Indian reservation was suffering from a terrible stomachache that wouldn't go away. Seeking out the tribe's shaman (medicine man), he asked for help.
The shaman, after listening to the missionary's symptoms, goes into a brief trance. Waking, he tells the missionary that to be cured, he must take a small bite out of the tribe's sacred leather thong. This thong had been worn by a great tribal warrior of the past and was much revered as a vessel of the brave's courage and strength.
The missionary takes the shriveled leather pouch back to his camp. The thought of where the thong had rested and the ancient stains on it caused the missionary some unease.
But as a new spasm rocked his stomach, the missionary did as he had been instructed and placed his teeth on the ancient garment and bit off a small piece, which he dutifully swallowed with a grimace.
This practice continued for the next two weeks.
At the end of which, the missionary sought out the shaman again. The shaman asked whether the missionary now felt any better. To which the young man replied,

"No, the thong is gone, but the malady lingers on!"

ARTHUR AND THE DRAGON

A wandering missionary was caught in a torrential rainstorm in rural England. Soaked to the bone, tired and hungry, he finally noticed a roadside inn ahead called, 'Arthur & the Dragon'.

Shaking the cold rain from his body the missionary enters the inn and asks the large forbidding woman at the front desk if there is any room at the inn.

The woman looks back at him without any seeming compassion and says,

"No."

"Perhaps I could get a little something to eat then?

She frowns and says,

"No."

"Then maybe just something warm to drink?"

The woman's frown turns into a grimace of disdain as she answers again,

"No."

About defeated, the missionary asks if he might be permitted one last request?

She looks at him menacingly.

"What?"

"May I please talk to Arthur?'

CARRYING A TORCH

A new missionary to darkest Africa asked his jungle guide if it was true that the wild animals would not attack you if you carried a torch at night?

"It depends on how fast you are carrying it."

CAMPING

Two missionaries named Alphonse and Dominic went camping in the forest. They found a nice level spot near a creek and set up their tent.

After a wonderful supper by the campfire, they put out the fire and climbed into their sleeping bags to meditate and go to sleep. Several hours went by and then Dominic nudged Alphonse and asked him to look up at the sky.

Alphonse's eyes gazed upward. The stars shone brightly in a celestial ballet above them. He heard himself describing aloud the beauty above them,

"God is all powerful. We are small and weak in comparison. His majesty shineth on us beyond all understanding. I lie here in awe and wonder."

To which Dominic replied,

"No. Not that you dummy! Somebody stole our tent."

BIGGEST LIE

A church missionary was visiting Southern Africa. As he took his morning walk he passed a group of young boys in an alley. The boys were bickering loudly and a small dog quivered with fright in their midst.

Fearing for the dog's safety, the missionary asked the boys what they were doing. The oldest of the boys looked around sullenly and said that they had found the lost little dog and each wanted to keep him. To decide who should get to keep the dog, they had decided to award the dog to the boy who could tell the biggest lie.

They were now taking turns telling preposterous stories and deciding whose lies were greater. And, they were having trouble agreeing which ones were the worse.

The missionary was visibly upset that these young men were wasting their talents in such an un-lofty pursuit and terrifying the small dog in the process. He raised his voice and harangued the boys about the pitfalls of lying.

Gesturing wildly with his arms for emphasis, he finished by stating that he was only trying to help their souls and that in his own youth an enlightened teacher had wakened him to the point that he was know able to avoid any untruth. He would never lie under any circumstances even if it meant his own death.

When the missionary finished speaking, the oldest of the boys sighed, looked over at his young friend, who held the puppy, and said.

"Okay, he wins - give him the dog."

STATE FAIR

A missionary boy was visiting a small town in New York. There he met two pretty Jewish sisters named Beth and Louise who lived next door. The young man screwed up his courage one day and asked Louise to go to the state fair with him.

Louise agreed and when they arrived, the boy asked his date what she would like to do first. She replied,

"Get weighed'

There just happened to be a carnival barker next to them at a weighing booth. Our missionary boy helped Louise up onto the weighing scale and the barker predicted she would weigh 120 lbs. The scale, when released read 109 lbs and the barker handed Louise a large stuffed bear as a prize for his inaccuracy.

They went on the Ferris wheel with the bear in-arm but Louise seemed to not be enjoying it. When the wheel stopped, the boy asked her what she'd like to do next. She replied,

"Get weighed".

The boy shook his head but found another weighing booth where Louise's weight was again estimated and when weighed, she won another teddy bear.

They each had some fast food and a drink and the boy asked again what else she would like to do.
He cringed a bit as she replied once more,

"Get weighed."

They were soon in possession of a third huge stuffed bear and the young man was getting tired of carrying them around. He took Louise home and dropped her and the bears off without so much as a goodbye kiss.

Louise's sister Beth met her at the door as the missionary disappeared down the street. Noticing how crestfallen her sister looked, she asked how the evening had gone. Louise looked sadly up and replied.

"Wousy."

HAIRCUTS

A young missionary was giving one of the grumpier older missionaries a haircut. His wrist slipped and he nicked the older missionary's ear causing it to bleed.

Apologetically, he asked for forgiveness and asked the older missionary if he could wrap his head in a warm towel.

"No," hissed the distressed older missionary,

"I'll just take it home under my arm...."

CLUMSY

There was a clumsy young missionary who was assigned various jobs at a South American mission church.

The first day he was making reading glasses. He slipped while working on the lens grinder and made a spectacle of himself.

The following day he worked in the kitchen helping the cook. But he backed into a meat grinder and got a little behind in his work.

The next day they decided to give him the simplest job at the mission which was taking fabric out of the loom and putting it in a basket.

There, things were going well until the loom for the upholstery fabric caught the sleeve of his shirt and pulled him violently inside. But don't worry... He's completely 'recovered' now.

CHIPS

Two missionaries were arrested for gambling in Texas. The judge asked how they could disgrace themselves and the church by gambling in public? The first missionary replied,

" But we weren't gambling for money judge."

"What were you playing cards for?"

"We were just playing for chips."

"Chips are the same as money. That'll be a $500. fine each. Next case."

The second missionary took his friend by the arm, handed the bailiff $1000. in chips and headed quickly for the door.

NEW MINISTERS

NEW SUIT

The young minister goes to a little tailor in town to pick up the new suit he had ordered. The tailor welcomes the minister and helps him into his new jacket. The sleeves of the jacket hang too low and the minister's fingers are barely visible. The tailor looks at the sleeves and tells the man to just hold his arms bent up at the elbows. Then the minister mentions that the jacket collar is now riding up on his neck. The tailor tells him to just hunch his shoulders up a bit.

Finally the tailor helps the minister into his new suit pants. The legs are uneven and drag on the floor. The man complains but the tailor has him walk with his knees bent to take up the slack. The minister has to leave to get back to the church on time.

Outside the church two young mothers notice the minister hurrying along in his new suit. The first says,

"The poor man ... all crippled up like that."

The second responds,

"Yes. But what a beautiful suit!"

ANOTHER SUIT

A recently ordained minister was proudly ordering a new suit from the town tailor. After the measurements the minister whispered to the tailor that he was sorry, but he wouldn't have the funds to pay for the new suit for another six months.

The tailor, who was part of the man's new congregation, whispered back that it was all right with him.

Relieved, the minister asked him when his new suit would be ready? To which the tailor replied,

"Oh, about six months."

SORE FOOT

An obese new minister was at the movies and as he was returning to his seat with a big bag of popcorn he asked a woman,

"Madam, did I step on your foot on the way out to the snack bar?"

"Why yes you did!"

"Good! Then this must be my seat."

FORE

Two new lady ministers were learning to play golf together. Rev. Ruth teed off first and they both watched in horror, as her shot took off sideways into a group of men on the adjacent fairway. The ball ricocheted off one man who fell to the ground grasping his hands to his groin in pain!
  Rev. Ruth rushed with her friend to help the poor man who still lay writhing on the ground in agony. Rev. Ruth got down on her knees next to the man and told him,

"I'm so sorry! Please let me help. I was a physical therapist before I entered the ministry and I think I can help you with your pain."

Without waiting for an answer she took the man's hands away from his groin, swiftly undid his zipper and placed her hands inside his pants gently cradling the groin area.

"There," she said, "doesn't that feel a bit better?"

"Why yes it does," he replied. "But I still think my finger's broken."

SLICE

The new minister was an avid but poor golfer. One day he took a huge swing at the ball, sliced it and watched as it sailed out of bounds and smashed through the windshield of a parked police car. The cop inside got out holding a chunk of the broken glass and walked over to the minister demanding,

"What are you planning to do about this?"

The minister timidly replied, "Change my stance?"

OLD MOVIE

The new minister saw his wife going into a movie theater with a tall, strange man. He told his friend that after carefully considering the matter, he had decided not to follow them.

"Why," asked his friend, "aren't you curious?"

"No, I've already seen the movie."

POST OFFICE

The new minister arrived at the post office early each morning to pick up the church mail. But no matter how early he arrived he found the envelopes damp and moist.

He asked the man who worked in the mailroom about the moisture problem.

The mailroom clerk just shrugged and told him there must be a lot of postage dew.

LONG DISTANCE CALLS

The newly ordained minister was also newly married. He had just begun his ministry with a small town congregation and money was in short supply.

When the couple's first phone bill arrived, the minister sat back in shock. His wife had run up over a hundred dollars in phone calls to her mother back in Tulsa. He took his young wife aside and explained their financial situation to her and emphasized how it would be necessary to write letters instead of calling her mother so often.

It was disconcerting that evening then, to hear his wife dialing on the phone just as he was working on his Sunday sermon. But he didn't want to jump to any conclusions as he called out,

"Darling, who are you calling?"

"It's okay dear. I'm just calling for the correct time."

The minister breathed a sigh of relief and was about to sink back into his chair when he had an awful thought and got up to hear his wife say,

"Hello Mom, what time is it?"

GEORGE BUSH'S NEW MINISTER

George Bush was still president when he was assigned a new presidential chaplain. George decided to give the new man increased responsibilities and sent him off to Afghanistan to bring the word of God to the multi-national allied forces there.

The new chaplain returned after six months and was waiting for George Bush in the presidential office. George saw the chaplain and asked,

"So, how did things go over there on your trip?"

The new chaplain replied honestly,

"Not so good. The sermons went fine. But three Brazillians were killed while I was there."

George Bush throws his hand to his forehead and goes,

"Oh no!"

George then dismisses the chaplain and goes back to the library in the White House where his wife finds him in a tizzy throwing books around and looking for a dictionary. She asks him what is wrong?

"For God's sake! Tell me - how much is a Brazillian?"

SPELLING

The newly arrived minister had fired the church secretary.
A friend asked the minister why he had fired the poor woman, who was well-liked in the congregation.

"She kept asking me how to spell the simplest words for her. This went on day after day. I couldn't take it any longer."

The friend nodded in understanding.

"Yes, I can see how that could be very annoying."

"Annoying isn't the half of it. It was positively embarrassing to have to keep saying, 'I don't know' all the time!"

OWIE

A new minister had just finished the Sunday sermon and was greeting members of his church outside afterwards. A little girl and her family came by and the little girl kept staring at the minister with a concerned look on her face. The new minister stooped over and asked the little girl if something was the matter?

She had one thumb in her mouth and with the index finger of her other hand she pointed at the minister's white collar and asked,

"Do... do you have an owie?"

The minister smiles at the little girl and slowly takes off his white collar to show it to her saying,

"See, its not a bandaid, it is just a special collar I wear. I don't have an owie."

The little girl looks intently at the man's neck and seeing no wounds starts to relax. She fingers the pure white collar and notices some fancy printing on the reverse side. She is too young to read and asks,

"What's these?"

The minister smiles some more and explains that the letters on the back of his collar are his neck size and a special printed blessing. Would she like to guess what the blessing says?

The little girl looks at her mother who nods her head that it is okay to guess. So she uses the extent of her slight knowledge of the world and other collars she's seen, as she scrunches up her face and guesses,

"Is it, 'Kills fleas and ticks for up to six months'?"

FIERY SERMONS

A new Pentecostal minister had been gradually losing membership in his church. Not being able to figure out why, he took a folio of his most recent sermons to the most senior minister in the region and asked if he should be 'putting more fire' in his sermons.

The older (and wiser) man looked through the sermons and offered just these words of advice,

"No. I think you should be doing just the opposite."

THREE NOTES

The new minister received a package from the former minister along with a letter explaining that the package contained that minister's accumulated wisdom from his years of experience at that church. It stated that if trouble presented itself, the new minister should use the enclosed envelopes numbered one to three for assistance.

The new minister tucked the package away and didn't give it much thought until the following spring when the church's tithing took a sudden dip. He pulled the envelope numbered 'One' from the package and opened it.

Inside was the advice that if tithing dipped,

"Blame the finances on me. I 'm not around anyway and it won't bother me."

The minister took the envelope's advice and his congregation grumbled but tithing briefly picked up.

Within a few months the tithing was again dropping. The new minister picked out the envelope numbered 'Two'. Inside was the message,

"Blame the finances on the wealthier members of the congregation. They are rich and it won't bother them as much."

The new minister did as the letter directed. The wealthier members grumbled but again tithing picked up for a while. Before summer was over the church till was again empty.

The new minister turned in desperation to the third envelope. Inside it he read,

"It's now time to be writing out three more envelopes."

TURBULENCE

A new minister was taking a cross-country flight to California when the plane ran into some severe in-flight turbulence. The turbulence got even worse and several of the younger passengers were getting frightened.

The stewardess noticed the minister's collar and asked if there was anything the minister could use from his church experience in this moment of crisis to help out.

The minister thought for a second, borrowed the hat from the passenger next to him and took up ...a collection.

DINNER ALONE

     A new young Minister was having dinner by himself at a new restaurant that had just opened near the church. He couldn't fail to notice as a gorgeous blond woman was seated at the table directly across from him. The blond smiles back at him and places her napkin demurely in her lap.

     The young minister is slightly embarrassed and looks away. Then he hears a loud sneeze and looks up to see the blond woman holding her nose. Gently rolling across the floor toward him is a glass eye.

     The minister reaches down and retrieves the glass orb and returns it to the blond woman. The woman pops the eye back into its socket and thanks the young minister saying,

"Thank you so much. I'm so sorry.... Please, let me buy you your meal for your kindness."

     The minister agrees and joins the young woman at her table. They have a wonderful meal together and enthusiastically talk about their lives and shared spiritual values.

     After paying for everything, the blond invites the minister to her home for lunch the next day so that they can continue their conversation. The minister hesitates for a second, but then agrees to meet her.

     Arriving at the blond woman's home the next day, the minister admires the small older house with beautiful flowers in front and a garden in back. A nice fire is in the fireplace and there are fresh-cut flowers on the table.

     He sits down to a gourmet meal that the woman has prepared by herself and they effortlessly continue their conversation as they eat. Everything seems so perfect.

     After dessert, the minister looks at the blond and says with obvious interest,

"You know, you really are the perfect woman. Attractive, intelligent, a wonderful homemaker and cook. How is it that you have never married? Are you this nice to everyone you meet?"

"Oh NO," she replies with a coy smile,
"You just happened to catch my eye."

DATING

An attractive young divorcee had fallen madly in love with our new minister. She took him aside after services and asked if there was any way they could see each other in a more 'passionate' way?

He responded loudly,

"What's the matter with you? Do you want to spend your time sneaking around and spending time in sleazy motel rooms? Is that what you really want?"

The woman looked down with shame and acknowledged,

"No. Of course not."

To which he replied,

"Well, they were ONLY suggestions."

TOUNGE-TIED

A new minister was leading a weekend prayer meeting. He raised his hands to Heaven and invited the Spirit of Jesus to move through his church and touch them with His Presence. Members of the church audience began reaching their arms skyward to invite the Spirit in. Soon people began to move with Spirit, talking in tongues, writhing in the aisles and shouting,

"Alleluia!".

The minister let the Spirit move and as people returned to their seats, he continued with his lesson saying,

"My brothers and sisters. Today our lesson regards the commandment 'I will not covet my neighbor's wife.' Yes, that great admonition against adultery. I suspect there may be some amongst us that have fallen to this temptation and if there are MAY DERE TONGUES CLEAVE TO THE WOOFS OF DERE MOUF."

ICE FISHING

A recently ordained minister was assigned to a church in northern Michigan. The young man had enjoyed fishing as a young boy in Florida. When he heard that there was something called ice fishing here in Michigan, he decided to give it a try.

He borrowed an ice auger and some fishing gear from the senior minister and headed out to a small pond alone. Trying to be careful of his footing, the young man augured a hole into the ice. He set out his gear and was just sitting down when a deep powerful voice came from above.

"There are no fish under the ice."

The minister jumped up at the sound of the voice and looked all around him. But there was no one there. A bit cautiously, he returned to his seat next to his gear. The voice from above spoke again.

"There are no fish under the ice."

The astonished man jumped up, looked around once more and asked loudly,

"Is that you God?"

"No," came the voice, "This is the rink manager."

DEAD ROOSTER

A new minister was driving through rural Alabama when he turned a blind corner too quickly and smashed through a flock of chickens on the road. He stopped and went back to survey the mass of feathers on the road. A few of the chickens were injured but the rooster amongst them was stone cold dead.

The minister picked up the rooster's limp body and took it to the nearby farmhouse where he knocked on the door. When the lady of the house answered, he confessed,

"I'm sorry. I have accidentally killed your rooster and I'd like to replace him for you."

The woman looked at the dead rooster and then locked her eyes onto the minister as she replied,

"That'll be fine by me I guess," she said eyeing him from top to bottom. "I guess you can just take yourself around to the hen house in the back. Them chickens be waiting!"

EXERCISE

The new minister at the church was very bright but also very lazy. The man's weight had increased over a hundred pounds in less than a year. The senior minister decided to intervene and took the grossly obese man aside.

In his best conciliatory tones he told the young man how much he was appreciated by everyone in the congregation but, how much more effective he might be if he just lost some weight. He would then feel better about himself and be able to participate in more of the church's activities.

The rotund young minister looked up from his couch and explained that exercise didn't 'suit' him. Running hurt his feet, walking bothered his knees and he didn't believe in competition so, most sports were definitely out.

The senior minister wasn't ready to let it go that easily and tried to think of the least difficult form of exercise.

"How about swimming then - even if you just get in the pool regularly, the activity would help melt some pounds off and improve your figure."

The massive young minister blinked his eyes for a second before rejoining,

"Reverend, I don't know that to be a fact - haven't you ever seen a Whale?"

(That same young minister had to take a leave of absence for health reasons later that year - he caught pneumonia while standing in front of the refrigerator.)

I GET NO RESPECT

The new minister goes into the hardware store to buy some rat poison.
The counter girl asks
"Should I wrap it up, or do you want to eat it here?"

The new minister was kidnapped while visiting the Middle East.
The gunmen sent a ransom note home along with a piece of the minister's finger. The congregation sent it back along with a message saying they needed more proof.

DEMOCRACY

Four Russian ministers had recently immigrated to the United States. The men decided to meet together each week to read the Bible and discuss theology. One of these 'discussions' led to a disagreement between the men and the oldest minister had decreed that, to keep the peace, they would try in the future to be more democratic and abide by the majority's opinion in each scriptural interpretation.

This sounded fair, but it upset the youngest of the ministers. Though the youngest, he had attended university and felt that intellectually, he was much more capable than the older men who seemed 'locked' into the old ways. Almost every 'discussion' ended with him disagreeing with the other ministers and him being voted down three to one.

The youngest minister tried to swallow his pride but it finally reached a boiling point one day when the other ministers kept insisting that there was no possibility that Jesus' teachings could have any interpretation other than their own. Again, he was voted down three to one when he tried to persuade them to keep an open mind on the subject.

In desperation, the young minister cast his arms skyward and appealed to God directly.

"Oh, God. Please hear my heart as I ask you to send us a sign that you are listening and that there is some truth in my words about Jesus."

The beautiful sunny day turned dark as black clouds obscured the sky.

"Look, Look." cried the young minister, "God is giving us a sign that I am correct."

The other ministers disagreed and pointed out that clouds often form on warm summer days and this was just an act of nature, not God.

"Please God, Give us a greater sign that they may know."

The sky got darker and lightening bolts flashed around them hitting and destroying the nearest tree. But the older ministers were not impressed and insisted it was just part of an ordinary storm.

The young minister started to call forth once more for a sign that they would not fail to recognize, but his plea was interrupted by a deep voice from the sky itself.

"He is right! This is the word of your Lord and God."

The clouds began to dissipate as the four ministers looked skyward in rapt amazement. Then the oldest minister cleared his throat and announced.

"Well, I guess that makes it three to two..."

WISHES

A young new minister had just married the beautiful leader of his church choir. They were honeymooning at a nearby lake resort and the minister was showing his new bride how to skip rocks across the placid lake's surface.

The young woman was determined to please her new husband. She took the flat rock he handed to her and unleashed it with all her strength toward the nearby water.

Regrettably, there was an expensive vacation home located next door and her energetic throw took an errant turn and the stone smashed loudly through its large picture window.

Aghast, the minister tried to comfort his now- sobbing wife. He explained that they would go up to the house together and explain exactly what had happened, that it was an accident, and that they would make amends.

So, the two of them went to the neighbor's house and knocked at the large impressive front door.

A deep but friendly voice answered,

"Please come in."

The couple entered the house and was appalled at the damage visible around them. Not only was the huge picture window shattered, but also the stone had continued into the house destroying a mirror and smashing a beautiful old antique bottle resting on a table nearby.

A rotund white-bearded man sat amongst the destruction peacefully looking at the frightened couple and asking,

"Are you the ones responsible for this?"

The young minister stepped forward and replied,

"Yes. But, it was an accident and we wish to pay for any repairs."

Yet at the same time he was mentally adding up the extent of the costly damage and fingering his thin wallet. The minister was surprised then, as the portly, bearded gent rose from his seat and welcomed him with a warm handshake and the words,

"No Apology is necessary. It is I who must thank you!
You see I am a powerful genie who has been trapped in that bottle for over two hundred years. You have set me free and as a reward I am allowed to grant three wishes. I will grant you each one of the wishes, but if you don't mind, I will keep one for myself."

The relieved minister looked at the benevolent genie and thought hard for a moment before asking,

"Can you grant me a million dollars every year so that I can do good works for the community and our church?"

The genie smiled and said,

"It is done. The money is all ready on it's way. And I will also see to it that you have a long and healthy life from which to do your good works." And, looking at the wife he asked,
"And what does your heart desire young woman?"

The minister's pretty blonde wife answered that she had always had this dream about having beautiful vacation homes in countries around the world. These would be places where they could stay with their church friends and conduct retreats.
The genie answered, "As you speak the words, it is done. The titles for these luxury homes are being drawn up at this very moment. And, I will see to it that they remain safe places for you and your friends."
The grateful young couple hugged themselves in gratitude for their remarkably good fortune. Then, they remembered their new genie friend.... and together, they asked,

"And what is it that you will use your wish for Genie?"

The genie now seemed a little shy and sad as he replied,

"I am not allowed to grant my own wish, but only to ask it aloud. I have been alone in my bottle for a very long time. My wish is for the company of a beautiful young woman for just one evening. And I would ask that your wife be the one to do me this great honor?"

The young minister looked at his wife and she looked back at him. the genie had done so much for them and he seemed like a gentle trustworthy type. The wife nodded her head and the minister replied for both of them,

"I love my wife and I know she loves me. We are very grateful to you genie. And if her company will bring you happiness, I give my permission for her to spend the evening with you."

His wife also nodded her assent and the minister placed his wife's hand into the hand of the now- glowing genie. With a kiss to his wife's cheek, he backed out the door and told her he would see her soon.
Alone with the genie, the young wife now felt a bit unprepared. What would this genie want from her in their time together? A glint now shown in the genie's eyes as he looked carefully at his younger companion.
Her mouth dropped open in shock as the genie started removing his robe – there was nothing under it - and then he moved closer! She tried to pull away but the genie was very strong and pulled her to him. Their struggle ended on a nearby couch where the genie made love to her. This love-making continued on and on. The genie seemed insatiable.
Finally, after four hours together, the genie took a break and looked

into the exhausted wife's eyes and asked her how old she and her husband were.

"We're thirty-five," she responded breathlessly.

"Really?" he answered.

" And you still believe in Genies?"

SMALL BOY

A new minister is walking down the street one day. He sees a small boy jumping up and down on the front porch of a house. The youngster is obviously struggling to reach the doorbell but he looks about jumped-out. The kindly minister takes pity on the poor little chap and walks over to help out.

The little boy looks leery as the minister approaches but the man puts a smile on his face and tells the boy there is nothing to worry about - he just wants to assist him. The small boy is still wary but he allows the minister to hoist him up by the waist until he is able to reach the doorbell.

The small boy reaches out and gives the doorbell a solid ring and then turns to smile back at the helpful man. The new minister asks,

"Is this your house young man?"

"Nope."

"Is it one of your little friend's houses?"

"Nope."

"Is it some message you need to deliver?'

"Nope."

"Well, what is it that happens when someone answers the door?"

"We run like Heck!"

NEW CHURCH

The minister had just finished his seminary training and had been assigned to open a new church in Australia. He arrived and found the large room that had been rented for the use of the church. It was clean, modern and had plenty of seats in front of a makeshift altar.

The minister unpacked and made himself comfortable. He waited around a bit not knowing what to do next as it was only Tuesday and services weren't scheduled until Sunday. He waited some more and then flipped the sign on the window to say OPEN in the hopes that someone might drop by early out of curiosity.

Sure enough, only an hour had gone by and he saw a man looking outside at the front of the church. The church looked so deserted, the minister decided he would try to make it and himself look busier by making some phone calls. He didn't have anyone to call but the phones weren't working yet either so he just picked up the receiver and pretended to talk.

The stranger outside wandered in the door and the minister waved him over as he pretended to talk to the bishop. After a few minutes of this pretense, the minister put the receiver down and welcomed the stranger to the new church. The man seemed a bit uncomfortable and the minister asked if there was anything troubling him? The man huffed a short cough and said,

"Err... I'm just here to connect your phone Guv.."

JOB SECURITY

Our new minister thought he was doing a great job until the end of the first year when he got his new business cards.
They all sported a blank space where he could write in his name.

CHURCH MEMBERS

SONS

At a church picnic three women are talking about their eldest sons. The first woman says,

"My oldest boy is an elder of the church. Whenever he walks into church everyone gets silent.'"

The second woman smiles smugly and shares that her eldest son is a minister. And that whenever her son walks into the church everyone stops and they say,

"Oh Reverend."

The third woman looks at the other two and rolls her eyes. Then she shares that her eldest son is seven feet tall and weighs five hundred pounds.

"When my son walks into church everyone stops, shakes their head and says,

'Oh my God!'"

ASHES TO ASHES

A minister was visiting a young woman who had recently moved into his congregation. In the woman's living room, the minister noted a beautifully carved vase filled with ashes. The minister asked about the vase and the young woman replied,

"Oh, Those are my father's ashes."

The minister recovered quickly and apologized for any insensitivity explaining,

"I'm so sorry, I didn't know your poor father had passed on."

To which she replied,

"He hasn't. He's just too damn lazy to go into the kitchen for an ashtray."

STINGY BROTHERS

Two old and stingy twin brothers belonged to the same church. The brothers had squirreled away a fortune during their lifetimes, lived in opulence but given very little to their neighbors or the church. Each was known to drop only a single dollar into the collection plate as it passed each Sunday.

One day one of the brothers became very ill and then he died the next day. His twin sought out the minister to arrange a funeral for his dear departed brother. The arrangements were made and paid-for and then the remaining brother wrote out a $100,000. check payable to the church.

"What is this for," asked the surprised minister.

"It is a donation to the church. But only on the condition that at the funeral, you must tell everyone present that my brother was a saint."

The minister looked at the leering evil-look on the remaining brother's face. He was trying to buy the church's good graces for all his brother had failed to do during his lifetime. But, the church was in dire need of the funds and the minister forced himself to shake the man's hand to seal the deal. The minister then rushed to the bank to deposit the check.

The following week, a huge funeral took place at the church for the deceased twin. When everyone was gathered, the minister got up to speak.

"I'd like everyone to know that the body resting before us is that of a horrible man who despised his neighbors, neglected his church and lived a filthy greedy life. But.... compared to his brother, this man was a Saint."

LONE RANCHER

On a cold wintry Sunday only one rancher showed up for the service. The minister told him,

"I guess we won't have a service today."

The rancher replied,

"If only one of my cows shows up at feeding time, I still feed it."

The shamed minister apologized and delivered a full service for the man. At the end he asked the rancher if he was satisfied? The rancher replied,

"Well Reverend, if only one of my cows shows up, I don't feed it the whole bale!"

WHISTLING DOCTOR

A member of our congregation was a practicing obstetrician at the local hospital. He still felt awkward while examining the private parts of his female patients. To cover his embarrassment he had developed the habit of softly whistling during the exams.

It was a bit strange one day when the minister's wife appeared on his table and he had to start the required pelvic exam. He tried not to think and instead just gently whistled as he did with all his other patients.

His embarrassment returned however when the minister's wife broke out laughing.

"I'm sorry," he said. "Am I tickling you?"

"No." she replied still giggling. "But that tune you are whistling sounded so familiar."

It was then he realized that the tune he had been whistling was familiar. He slapped his head as the words of the tune came back to him,

"I wish I was an Oscar-Meyer wiener!"

SUPERMARKET FATHER

Phillip was one of the church's board members. One day he is in the supermarket and notices an attractive blond woman waving to him across the produce aisle. She looks familiar but he can't place her. As she gets closer he asks,

"I'm sorry. You look familiar – do I know you?"

To which she smiles and replies,

"Yes. You are the father of one of my children."

Phillip's mind races back in time with horror to his bachelor days.

"Oh no," he says, "are you the stripper I made love to on that pool table at the fraternity house?"

"No, she replies indignantly, "I am your daughter's fourth grade teacher."

MURDERESS

The prison chaplain asked the condemned murderess about her crime:

"You poisoned your husband's coffee and then sat down at the table with him and watched him drink it. Didn't you feel any remorse or pity?"

"Well, I guess there was a moment when it did bother me a bit."

"And when was that?"

"When he reached over for that second cup."

CHURCH VISITOR

A gentleman from out of town was visiting our church one Sunday. He noticed that our attractive Sunday school teacher wasn't wearing a wedding ring and after the service he asked her out on a date. She agreed and that night he picked her up for a dinner date.

At the restaurant they enjoyed a good meal together and he invited her to join him for a cocktail. She demurred saying,

"Oh no. What would my Sunday school class think?"

On their way back to the car he pulled out a cigarette and offered her one. Again she refused saying,

"Oh no. What would my Sunday school class think?"

Once they were in the car he decided to make one more proposition asking,

"Would you like to come over to my motel room with me?"

He was a bit surprised as she acquiesced replying that,

"Yes, that would be nice."

They spent that night romantically involved and in the morning he had to ask her,

"And what do you think your Sunday school class would say about our evening together?"

"Oh, the same thing I always tell them: You don't have to smoke or drink to have a good time."

SMOOTH TALKER

A rather slow, shy, single minister named Reverend Clem had just been transferred to a new congregation where one of the local spinsters had taken a romantic interest in the young man. The following was overheard at the annual church picnic when the lady managed to get herself alone with the reverend.

"Reverend Clem, Do you think I'm pretty?"

"Ahhh....yup."

"Reverend Clem, do you think I'm fun to be around and make you happy?"

"Ahhh....yup."

"Reverend Clem, do you think my lips are as soft as flower petals and my eyes as enchanting as an evening sunset?"

"Ahhh Yup."

"Oh Reverend Clem! You do say the most romantic things."

CRUISE SHIP

Our church organized a cruise ship vacation. But on the first night at sea huge waves caused seasickness and pink anti-nausea pills were handed out. The next morning icebergs were sighted and purple anxiety pills were handed out. By the third night everyone on board was marooned.

PHOTOGRAPHY

A lady from the church, who was a photographer, spent all her time praying alone in her dark room.
She was asked why she didn't join the rest of the congregation for prayers in the chapel?
She replied that the dark room was more appropriate because her favorite prayer was that 'someday her prints would come.'

JAIL

Our minister was visiting one of his congregation in the state correctional institute. The man had been convicted of burglary in twenty-one different cases. The old minister admonished the man saying,

"Aren't you ashamed of yourself.? Twenty-one different people you've hurt. Twenty-one <u>convictions</u>. Won't you ever learn? What do you have to say for yourself?"

"Reverend, Haven't you yourself said that we shouldn't be ashamed of our convictions."

CROSS WORDS

A member of the church's faithful had recently died. And, as the man was a crossword puzzle devotee during life, the minister had him buried six feet down and three across.

RAINY NIGHT

Limpy and Loopy were caught out in the forest during a terrible storm. They were soaking wet and lightening was crashing all around them as they found the main road and started back to their home. A large truck turned the corner and was unable to stop before it struck Limpy and knocked him to the ground. The truck driver continued on without looking back.
Loopy held his friend's head up out of the puddle and knowing his friend was dying said he would go to get their minister. Limpy grabbed his hand and said,

"No. Go get me a rabbi instead."

"But Limpy, you are a Baptist. Surely you'd prefer I get the minister."

"No. Get me a rabbi. I'd never ask our minister to come out on a night like this."

THE BLIND WILL SEE

A blind boy named Jose was taken to see a famous Christian healer. He was seen and blessed by the holy man and upon his return to the United States found out that he was now able to see.

His grateful family tried to make up for all the sights Jose had missed during his years of blindness. His parents took him to Disneyland and then his uncle offered to take him to his first baseball game.

When they got back from the game the boy was crying. His concerned parents asked him if everything was all right?"

"Oh yes. It was the most wonderful thing. Even better than Disneyland."

"Then why are you crying son?"

"Oh, it was the song. To think that many people care about me. It makes me cry."

"What song was that son?"

"You know. The one that starts, JOSE, CAN YOU SEE..."

GOD'S MEMORY

A very pious gentleman had just celebrated his 100th birthday. The man had attended the same church every day of his life since he had been a young boy. Now the members of the church were concerned because the old man was no longer in attendance.

The minister went to see the old man and found him home and in excellent health. He congratulated the man on his recent birthday but had to ask,

"Why do you no longer attend our church?"

"Well since you ask, I'll tell you Reverend. When I turned 80 years old I had already lived longer than any of my relatives and family. I expected God to take me home every day. When he hadn't by the age of 85, then 90 then 95 and now 100, I began to think He might have forgotten about me. And. now... I'm keeping a low profile ... just hoping He DOESN'T REMEMBER."

AEROPLANE RIDE

   The old Amish minister and his wife Rachel had just retired after serving in their small rural congregation for over fifty years. During that time they had never had time for any vacations, had watched every penny and donated any savings back to the community.

   Their first big trip in retirement was to the state fair. The old minister looked on in amazement at the unusual sights, rides and people all around them. His first pension check was recently cashed and the money was in his pocket.

   The biggest impression left on the old man was by a stunt pilot who flew overhead performing aerial acrobatics in the sky. The pilot ended his performance by landing on the fairgrounds next to a sign offering rides to the public.

   The old minister looked at the sign, looked at his wife and said,

"I'd sure like to take me a ride in that there Aeroplane."

   His wife Rachel, replied,

"Yes, but the sign says it is $40. for a ride. And $40. is $40."

   The old Amish man looks down dejectedly and follows his wife home.
   The following year the couple returns to the fair and again the old minister sees the airplane ride sign. He says,

"Rachel, I sure do still want that Aeroplane ride. If I don't do it soon, I'll soon be dead and never get the chance."

   Rachel again replies,

"That there Aeroplane ride still says $40.. And $40. is $40.."

   The old Amish man looks down again and is about to leave. But this time the plane's pilot has heard their conversation and steps forward to approach the elderly couple.

"Listen," he says, "I'd like to make a deal with you. I'll take you both up for a ride in my airplane. And the ride will be free if you can be quiet and not say a word. But if you say anything or even scream, you'll have to pay for the ride."

   The old Amish minister and his wife Rachel look at each other. Both nod their assent and the pilot helps them into the back seat of the old bi-plane. The plane takes off and the pilot goes through his entire repertoire of twists, barrel rolls and loops.

   Finally the pilot lands the plane and goes to congratulate the couple for not loosing their composure and yelling in the more severe maneuvers the way most young people did.

The old man's a bit shaky as he replies,

"Well I almost said something back in that last loop when Rachel fell out... But ..... $40. is $40...."

BETTER PLAN

A cantankerous old man confided in his minister one day that he could no longer take his wife's constant nagging. They couldn't afford to go through a divorce, so he had decided to poison her.

The minister was appalled and counseled the man that besides the spiritual ramifications, there was no poison that could not be detected and he would forfeit his own life when the police caught him.

He suggested that a better plan that might accomplish the same goal would be to have the old man make love to his wife ten times a day for at least eight weeks.

The old man shook his head at the instructions but agreed that he would at least give the minister's plan a chance.

After seven weeks the minister had not heard anything from the old man so he decided to visit the couple. The minister arrived and was shocked at the old man's appearance as he answered the door. The old man had shriveled almost completely away, looked twenty years older and now moved with a cane.

Then the old man's wife traipsed through in a bathing suit looking like a young woman again.

"My God," said the minister, "your wife looks wonderful."

The old man chortled and wheezed in reply,

"Yeah, the old bitty doesn't even know she's about to die!"

EXCUSES

Our minister stopped one of his congregants as he was exiting the church. He stared at the man with a baleful eye and accused him with,

"I heard that you went to the ball game last Sunday instead of coming to church."

"That's a lie," said the man - "and I have the fish to prove it!"

GOT GAS?

A group of church ladies who worked at a nursing home together were driving out of town to pick up a new patient at a retirement home. Before they could get to the rural address, their car ran out of gas.

A friendly farmer passed the women sitting on the side of the road praying. He stopped and offered to drain some gas from his tank for them. But, he had no can to drain the gas into and couldn't get his truck close enough to drain it to their tank directly.

One of the women rummaged through the car and found a large bedpan that they had intended to use with their new patients.

"Will this work, sir?"

"Sure will," replied the farmer. And he proceeded to drain a gallon of gas into the pan. When he had finished, he bid the ladies a good day and set off to finish his errands.

The ladies thanked the farmer and God for the gift and gently tipped the contents of the pan into the open cap of their gas tank.

At just this moment, a state trooper drove by and took notice of the odd sight. He stopped his car, backed up to the church ladies and hollered out to them,

"I don't think that's going to work ladies. But, I sure do have to admire your Faith!"

GAMBLERS

A well-known gambler had recently passed away and many of his Las Vegas friends were at the funeral. The minister read praises for their dead friend and concluded with,

"Randy is not really dead, he only sleepeth."

A voice from the back was heard to say,

"I've got a hundred bucks here that says he's dead."

MAKING BABIES

Little Reggie came home from school with a big smirk on his face. The minister's wife was visiting and asked him what he had learned at school.
He replied,

"How to make babies."

Reggie's mother and the minister's wife both blanched and only recovered from their shock when he added,

"First you drop the 'y' and then you add 'ies'.

TEDDY BEARS

A woman from the choir meets a former classmate at a church social. He tells her how he has been living in a cave for the past twenty years and has just recently returned to public life. He tells her he has gotten a job working the ring-toss at a local carnival. They enjoy talking together and she accepts his invitation to go back to his apartment to see his church music collection.
Arriving at his small one room apartment she notices the two huge bookcases on either side of his bed. One contains his religious books and the collection of church music. The other bookcase is covered in cute cuddly tteddy bears of all sizes with the larger ones on the top shelf.
The woman is impressed with the sweet sensitive nature of this man as he shows her his music collection. They talk some more sitting on the bed and soon they are kissing. She stays and after a night of passion with this sensitive, gentle man she gets up to go in the morning. The former classmate lies there watching her dress and she is tempted to ask,

"How was it, after all those years?"

He says,

"Help yourself to any of the bears from the bottom shelf."

HYPOCRITES

A farmer with a history of missing services for various reasons told the visiting minister that he never went to church anymore because there were just too many hypocrites there. The minister replied,

"There's always room for one more."

THE DIME

An unlucky man had gambled away all of his money. He had nothing to eat and only the clothes on his back. To make matters even worse, he had to use the bathroom desperately and the only restroom in the hotel had a pay toilet.

A visiting minister saw the distraught-looking man in the hotel lobby and asked him what the problem was. The man explained his dire need and the minister handed him a dime for the toilet.

The unlucky man thanked the minister and rushed off to the bathroom. There he found the stall unlocked and after attending to his 'business', decided to return to the hotel casino and used the dime in his hand on a slot machine.

It must have been a lucky dime because he hit an immediate jackpot. The man took his winnings to the blackjack table and proceeded to win a sum of a little over a million dollars.

A local newspaper heard about the man's story and wrote an article in the local paper about this amazing change of luck. With the story was the now-lucky man's offer to split his enormous winnings with his unknown benefactor.

The minister who had lent the man the dime read the story and realized that this must be God's answer to the needed funds for their church orphanage's new roof!

The next day the minister showed up at the address of the lucky man as it was listed in the paper. Knocking on the door, the minister waited patiently. Finally, the door opened. the now-lucky man opened it himself and looked into the minister's eyes.

"What do you want?'

"Don't you remember me? I'm the man who gave you the dime."

"Oh yeah. But you're not the right one.'

"What do you mean ' not the right one'?"

"Well, thanks for the dime. But I'm looking to reward the guy who left the stall open."

VEGETARIANS

Vegetarians feel that their diet makes them healthier and sometimes feel closer to God. But two vegetarian friends of mine started eating meat again. I asked them why?

"Because we were starting to tilt towards the sun".

One-Two-Three

A hard-bitten old widowed Amish farmer was driving his buggy home from church with his new young wife Rachel beside him. The old nag pulling the carriage was kind of ornery and refused to move forward at the next road intersection. The old farmer cussed at the horse and finally said,

"That's One!"

The horse turned its head around and then proceeded ahead. At the next intersection the horse paused to visit with another horse in the pasture next to the road. The old farmer flogged at the horse with the reins and yelled,

"That's Two!"

The horse gave in and moved forward again until they reached the neighbor's flower garden. Here the horse stopped completely and proceeded to munch the neighbor's flowers. The old Amish farmer's face was beet red as he screamed,

"That's Three!"

And with that, he leaped from the seat of the buggy, took his shotgun out from behind the seat and shot the poor horse dead on the spot. Rachel was shocked and upset by her new husband's behavior and told him,

"That was a stupid and cruel thing to do! Now how are we going to get the carriage back to the farm?"

The old farmer looked at his wife with eyes squinted almost closed and barked,

"That'll be One, Rachel."

AMISH ELEVATOR

An Amish boy went to the new regional shopping center for the first time with his father. They were amazed by all the wonderful new and unusual things they found there. In particular, they were puzzled by a set of shiny metal doors that kept opening and closing by themselves.
The child asked,

"What are these, father?"

The father had never seen anything like them before either and told his son:

"I don't know."

As the two of them stood there pondering the meaning of the doors, a heavy older woman in a wheelchair pushed the button on the wall, wheeled through the open shiny doors and disappeared as the doors closed after her.
Circular numbers above the doors lit up as they watched. They noticed the numbers seem to stop and then light up in reverse order. The doors opened again in front of them and a beautiful young blonde woman stepped out from behind and briskly walked away from the two staring men.
The father continued to follow the young woman with his eyes as he turned to whisper to his son.

"Go get thee thy mother!"

THE EDS

A woman we know went to a church retreat and met a Reverend Ed Snow. They were married six months later. She went alone to the church retreat the next year because her husband was out of town.
She met another minister named Ed Wilson this time. She didn't mention she was already married and they fell madly in love and wound up going to Las Vegas to get married.
Her friends didn't know what to say to her when she got back from her second honeymoon. She told them not to worry because her mother had always said that ...

"Two Eds are always better than one. "

REAR END

The young widow went to her minister to make arrangements for her husband's funeral. The minister looked through her request list and balked as he came to an item at the end asking,

"I understand everything on your list except this last item. Why in the world would you want to have your husband buried with his rear end sticking out of the ground?"

"Well," said the young woman, "its true that Ned and I didn't get along particularly well when he was alive. But I want to be a good wife and visit his grave regularly. And when I do, I'm going to want to have some place to park my bike."

VIVA LE DIFFERANCE

A young catholic boy was playing in his wading pool with the Protestant daughter of the next-door neighbor. The two kids were having a good time and the little girl suggested that they take their bathing suits off. The little boys eyes opened wide as the suits came off and he exclaimed,

"Wow, I didn't know there was THAT much of a difference between Catholics and Protestants!"

RAFFLE PRIZES

Three Lutheran ministers in Minnesota got together to plan a joint winter festival for their three church congregations. They decided that a church raffle would be a good way to raise the funds to pay for the festival. The big question was what type of prize should they offer in the drawing?

Reverend Olaf shared that last year, his church had offered free tickets to a Christmas play. The winning couple had seemed pleased but something different might be better this year.

Reverend Sven shared that his congregation had offered free lodging at the town's only hotel. But, until they offered indoor plumbing and got rid of the outhouse, something else might be better as a prize.

Reverend Lute just shook his head when it was his turn to share.

"Vell, I don't know dat I can 'elp. Lest Yere Ole's 'ardvare store donated dese toilet brushes. Vell Inger an her sisters won dem at de raffle. Ven I ask bout dem, she tol me de vas very nice, but she tinks de vill be goin back to usin de toilet paper."

MATERIALISM

A very wealthy member of the congregation was parking his new BMW convertible on the street in front of the church. As he got out of the car, a speeding truck came by passing too close to the curb and completely ripped the open door of the BMW from it's hinges.

The church's minister saw the truck speeding off and rushed over to help. He arrived to witness the owner screaming profanities at the truck driver and cursing the fact that his new BMW would never be the same again.

The minister was shocked by the man's language and attitude. Shaking his head in disgust, the minister upbraided the wealthy man by saying,

"Are you so lost in your materialistic views that you have forgotten where you are and the things that are most important?"

The wealthy man was still red in the face with anger and in his fury shouted back at the minister.

"How can you say such a thing? Didn't you see what happened? That *&%&$*!"

The minister responded with concern,

"My God man. Don't you even realize that your left arm is missing? It was ripped off in the accident and you're bleeding! Who cares about the condition of the car or the truck driver."

The car owner looks down for the first time and notices his missing limb and with unabated fury shouts up to heaven.

"Damn it all.... Not my new Rolex too!"

NEW MERCEDES

A man had just purchased his first Mercedes Benz and was so proud of it that he invited a priest, a minister and a rabbi to come by and bless the vehicle for him.

The priest sprinkled it with holy water and chanted a prayer in Latin.

The minister invoked the name of Jesus Christ and led them all in silent prayer.

The rabbi sang a psalm and then cut off the end of the tailpipe.

OLD SINNER

An old man totters on his cane quietly into the Saturday night confessional at Saint Joseph's church. Taking a seat in the confessional booth next to the priest, he begins to speak slowly,

"Father, I am ninety years old this week. I have a wonderful wife at home. We've been married seventy years and have five wonderful kids and twenty healthy grandchildren. Last week I went fishing by myself and there were four college girls camping nearby. I introduced myself to them and they invited me to stay at their campsite. That night I made love to all four of the girls and in the morning when I left they thanked me for the experience."

The priest harruphhed at this last part before speaking,

"You know it doesn't matter if the girls were willing. It is still a sin.
 Are you sorry for your sins?"

"What sins?"

"What do you mean 'what sins'? What kind of Catholic are you?"

"What kind of Catholic? I'm not Catholic at all. I'm a Presbyterian."

"Then why are you in here telling me all this?"

The old man smiled and said, "Because I'm telling everybody!"

TICKETS

An ambitious church deacon was selling tickets for the church benefit concert. He cornered an old tightwad and asked if he would like some tickets to the concert? The stingy old man recoiled a bit and said,

"I'm sorry, I don't think I'll be able to attend. But my 'Spirit' will be there with you."

The deacon smiled and pushed a ticket at the tightwad saying,

"Would your 'Spirit' like to sit in a five or ten dollar seat?"

BRIBERY

A married woman was nearly caught with her lover when her husband came home from work early. Looking around in panic, she hid her lover in the pantry closet. The lover thought he was alone until the unmistakable sound of breathing was heard behind him.

In the dim closet light, the lover was relieved to see that it was only the woman's young son. The little boy looked up at the lover and asked,

"It's awfully dark in here, isn't it mister?"

The lover tried to hush the boy and handed him $10 to stay quiet. But the little boy shook his head and said,

"That's not enuf."

The lover dipped into his pocket and handed the boy another $10.

"Still not enuf."

The lover pulled out his last $20 and handed it to the boy. The boy looked at the cash in his hand and nodded that he would be quiet.

The next day, the mother took her young son to the store and was shocked when she caught him pulling ten-dollar bills out of his pocket to buy candy. She asked where the money had come from but her son wasn't talking. Finally she grabbed him by the hand and pulled him out of the store saying,

"If you won't tell me, you'd better tell Reverend Goody, or you'll go to hell with the rest of the bad boys."

The mother drove them directly to the church and put her young son in the minister's office. The boy was terrified as he had never been in the minister's office. He turned with pleading eyes back to his mother but she angrily told him to stay there and wait.

Inside the dimly lit room, the boy looked as the minister took his seat across from him and glowered across the desk. He wasn't sure how to begin, so he just said,

"It's awfully dark in here, isn't it?

To which the minister dourly replied,

"Don't start with me again!"

FUNERALS

FUNERAL ANNOUNCEMENT

The widow Leary arrived at church early one Saturday morning shortly after her husband Ned had died. She asked the elderly minister,

"Reverend Greedy, I'd like to place an announcement in the church bulletin about my poor Neddy."

She handed the minister a two-paged typed memorial listing some of her husband's accomplishments. Rev. Greedy looked at the two pages and explained that there was only room left in the bulletin for eight words. The widow seemed stricken She looked at all the important things she wanted to say and finally wrote down, 'Ned is dead." The minister explained that she had five more words. She was overcome with grief and told Rev. Greedy to add the rest himself.

That night the minister misplaced the widow's list. He tried his best to remember something special about Ned. All he could recollect about Ned and his wife was that they had lived very frugal lives so, the final bulletin announcement he came up with read,

"Ned is dead. Good used truck for sale."

CALIFORNIA VACATION

Reverend Jackson left his home church in New Jersey to attend a church conference in California. He decided to stay an extra week and enjoy the sunny weather with his wife. At the end of the week he suffered a massive heart attack and was pronounced dead before he could get to the hospital.

His grieving widow had his body shipped back to New Jersey and the whole town showed up to pay its respects at the funeral. As people passed by the open casket, a friend of the family told the widow that it was a shame her husband had been taken by the Lord so early in his career but, at least she could remember how serene and marvelous he looked today.
The widow replied,

"You're right. I think that week of sun in California did him a world of good."

FUNERIAL CHANGES

An extremely agitated widow approached the minister who was scheduled to perform the funereal service for her husband that evening.

"Reverend, I just got back from the funeral home. They've put my dear Ned in a black suit. He looks so uncomfortable. The family in the next room had their man in Bermuda shorts and a Hawaiian shirt. Is there any way you could have Ned attired in something like that before the service tonight?"

The minister looked a bit irritated at the request but said he would contact the funeral home and try to honor her wishes.
That night the service took place as scheduled and Ned looked radiant in his casket wearing a bright Hawaiian Shirt and short pants. After the service and a beautiful eulogy the widow sought out the minister to thank him.

"Thank you so much Reverend. You don't know how much it meant for me to see Ned looking so virile and natural. I hope it wasn't too much trouble?"

"Nonsense," replied the minister, "it wasn't easy because the funeral home was very busy today. And they didn't have many spare clothes either. But, the director owed me a favor ... so, instead of trying to change Ned, I managed to get him to ... switch the heads."

EPITAPHS

Our minister and a colleague were attending the funeral of another minister who had just passed away. Looking down at the coffin, our minister asked his colleague what he would like to have said about him at his own funeral?
The man thought for a second before answering that,

"I WOULD HOPE THAT THEY SAY I WAS A WONDERFUL TEACHER AND A FAITHFUL SERVANT OF GOD WHO TOUCHED THE LIVES OF MANY."

And how about you?

"LOOK, HE'S MOVING!"

FUNEREAL PROCESSION

A devout, married woman was on her way home from church when she noticed a funereal procession on it's way down the center of the street. Three long black hearses were slowly rolling down the street with a solitary woman in black mourning dress right behind them.

A large Doberman pinscher dog followed the woman in black on a black leash. Further behind the dog trailed a long line of women all walking with heads bent in single file.

Our churchwoman was moved by the solemnity of the group and when it momentarily paused at a red light, she seized the moment to pay her condolences to the poor widow in black. At the same time, she inquired about the long length of the procession - her husband must have been much loved.

The widow explained,

"The first hearse is for my husband. He had tried to bring two strange women home while I was gone but was attacked and killed by my dog." "The second and third hearses are for his two mistresses. They tried to help protect my husband, but my dog sensed that they were sinners and turned on them and killed them as well."

A brief meaningful pause occurred as the two women looked into each other's hearts. Then our church lady asked softly,

"May I borrow your dog?"

The answer,

"Get in line."

HEAVEN

SOFTBALL IN HEAVEN

Two eighty-year-old friends named Jo and Jean found out that Jo was terminally ill and would be passing soon. Jean visited Jo every day to comfort her and in passing made an unusual request saying,

"Jo, we have been friends for almost sixty years – ever since we met playing high school softball. We played in college together and for our company softball team. I want you to promise me one thing. If there is any way, when you get to the other side, you must let me know whether they have softball teams in Heaven?"

Jo responded,

"Yes Jean. If it is possible, I will find a way to let you know."

The following day Jo passed into the great beyond. The night after Jo's funeral, a flash of light woke Jean in her bedroom and her old friend's voice called out to her,

"Jean, Jean, can you hear me?"

Jean was now fully awake as she replied,

"I hear you. Is that you Jo?"

"Yes Jean, its me. I'm here in Heaven now and it is so beautiful. I've come back to tell you that there are softball teams here in Heaven. But there is some good news and bad news about them."

"Oh Jo, thank you so much for letting me know. Please tell me the good news first."

"Well the weather here is always perfect and games are never cancelled. Better yet, we are all young again and all of our old friends are here and waiting for us to play."

"That's wonderful! And the bad news?"

"You are going to be our starting pitcher this coming weekend."

EATING IN HEAVEN

Percy was a good and generous person during his earthly life before he passed away. Jesus himself greeted him at the gates to Heaven and took him on a quick tour of the heavenly realm. Jesus then asked Percy if he were hungry?

Percy hadn't given it much thought but answered,

"I could eat a little something."

So Jesus conjured up a can of beans, opened it and they shared it. While eating his beans, Percy happened to look down and far below them he could see into the open gates of Hell. He was surprised to notice that the inhabitants of Hell seemed to be sitting down for a meal of their own around a huge wooden table covered with what appeared to be a full turkey dinner.

The next day Jesus came by to visit with Percy again and after some conversation asked Percy if he were hungry? Percy was indeed a lot hungrier today and told Jesus,

"Yes, I could eat."

Jesus conjured up a can of tuna this time, opened it and they shared the contents. Again Percy was tempted to look down. There in Hell the many souls and devils were gathered around a huge table covered with fried chicken, gravy, potatoes, vegetables and a wide array of desserts.

The following day around noon, Jesus again arrived to visit. The visit lasted a little longer than usual and when Jesus asked him if he was hungry, Percy quickly replied.

"Yes. And I might even say I'm famished."

It was with an obvious look of disappointment that Percy watched Jesus materialize another can of beans for them to share. Trying not to be too ungrateful, Percy asked Jesus,

"Jesus, I am very grateful to be here in Heaven with you as a reward for the good life I led on Earth. But I don't understand the meals of canned beans and tuna. I look down into Hell and they seem to be eating such huge elaborate meals. What gives?"

Jesus just laughed understandingly and explained,

"Now Percy, with just the two of us here, does it make any sense to cook?"

EATING RIGHT

An elderly married couple were killed in a crash after celebrating their 70th Anniversary. They had lived long and healthy lives mainly because the wife had been devoted to fitness and proper diet for both of them. They arrived in heaven where Saint Peter gave them both a short tour.

"This is the mansion where you will live," said Saint Peter. It was like a castle with vaulted ceilings, fifty oversize rooms decorated extravagantly, with a fireplace and a Jacuzzi in each room.

"Wow," said the old man, "this is quite a place. How much is this going to cost?"

To which Saint Peter replied,

"This is heaven, it is free."

Strolling outside, they gazed in wonder at the beautiful gardens surrounding their new home. The old man watched as a golf ball flew by in the distance. He asked Saint Peter if there was a golf course nearby.

"Yes," said Saint Peter. "There are two championship golf courses that back right up to your property."

"Whew," wheezed the old man. "And what are their green fees like?'

Saint Peter answered,

"This is heaven. They are free."

Walking over to the nearest course clubhouse, the couple marveled at the enormous array of delicious cooked foods adorning the tables inside.

"That's quite a spread!" said the man "How much to eat?"

"I don't think you quite understand yet," said Saint Peter, "this is heaven. Everything is free. And beside that, you can eat as much as you want of anything you want and you will never get fat or sick."

For some reason the old man got upset at this. He threw his hat down on the floor and stomped on it angrily. Spitting on the floor, he shrieked at his wife to leave him alone. Saint Peter tried to help his wife calm the old man down.

"What's wrong? Is there something about heaven you don't like?"

The old man was still fuming, but he managed to fix a baleful stare at his wife as he yelled,

"It's all your fault old woman. You and your stinking bran muffins! If it hadn't been for them, I know I could have been up here twenty years ago!"

LORD'S PRAYER

The ghost of Colonel Sanders arrives in Heaven and request's an audience with Jesus. The ghost says he has a deal to offer Jesus to help solve some of the church's financial problems. Jesus is a bit leery of this strange offer but the earthly church does need money so he asks to hear about the 'deal'.

The white-haired ghost smiles and explains the proposition,

"Well Jesus, here's the deal. My old KFC franchises have been slowing down a bit since I passed on. I figured it might help some if you could just change the words of The Lord's Prayer a bit to say, GIVE US THIS DAY OUR DAILY CHICKEN. We'd sell a lot more chicken and we'd split all the profits with the church fifty-fifty. What do you say?"

Jesus is aghast at the thought and replies haughtily,

"The Word of God cannot be changed and it is certainly not for sale!"

The old white-haired ghost of Colonel Sanders just scratches his bearded chin and offers up,

"What if we make it a seventy-thirty split? That might be as much as a billion dollars a year for the church. What do you say - have we got a deal?"

Jesus hesitates a bit at the mention of the 'billion' and says to the ghost that he will get back to him with an answer the next day. They shake hands and the ghost leaves.

The next day Jesus calls in the angelic head of heavenly finances and tells the angel to prepare for some good news and some bad news. The finance director asks for the good news first. Jesus says,

"I have found a new way for the Church to increase its resources by a billion dollars a year."

The finance director is duly impressed and then remembers there is some bad news as well. He asks to hear it.

Jesus replies,

"We are losing the Wonderbread account."

HEAVENLY MEDICINE

There was an explosion in a hospital and three doctors were killed. They arrived at Heaven's Gate and were met by Jesus. Jesus asked the first man what his specialty was at the hospital. The man replied,

"Obstetrics."

"Okay," said Jesus. " You may enter."

Jesus asks the next man what his specialty was?

"Orthopedics."

"Okay. You may enter."

The third physician explains that he was a General Practitioner at the hospital.

"Sorry," says Jesus, " you can take two aspirin and come back again tomorrow."

PROFESSIONS

Three recently deceased friends met as they reached Heaven together. One was a doctor, another an engineer and the third a politician. They welcomed each other and then tried to decide whose profession was the oldest.

"Well," said the doctor. "Without medical knowledge I'm sure Eve would never have been created from Adam's rib."

The engineer replied that even before Adam and Eve there had to be order created from the chaos. And that was definitely an engineering job.

The politician puffed up his chest and explained,

"Yes. But even before that - who do you suppose it was that created the chaos?"

HEAVENLY STORES

Picky Priscilla dies and goes to Heaven after living a long lonely life as a spinster. A female angel appears to her and tells her that there are many wonderful stores here in Heaven.

"There is even a store filled with millions of eligible men from whom to pick a husband."

The angel then takes Picky Priscilla to a huge multi-level storefront labeled 'MEN'. Inside there is a sign that explains that the store has five levels and that everyone must start on the ground floor. There was a limit of one man to each shopper and if you didn't find what you liked on one floor, you could take the elevator up to the next floor.

But, the elevator only operated in one direction (UP) so, once you left a floor, you could not return to it.

Eager to get started, Picky Priscilla starts looking around at the men on the first floor. They seem nice but are nothing special. She decides to look at the men on the second floor and takes the elevator up. Here there are even more men and these men seem more prosperous and well dressed.

'Pretty Good', thinks Priscilla but I'm curious about the third floor.

On the third floor the men are all nice, prosperous and well dressed. But these men are also extremely good looking.

'Wow', thinks Priscilla, 'this is great!' But some part of her still wonders if they could be even better on the fourth floor.

On the fourth floor Priscilla can hardly believe it. Every one of the men is nice, well-dressed, handsome, likes to do housework and cooks as well! Priscilla is about to choose one but her eyes keep being pulled to the open elevator door. How could she choose one of these men when there might be something even better on the fifth floor? So she waves her good-byes to the lonely men on the fourth floor and takes the elevator up one more time.

The elevator door slides open at the fifth floor and Priscilla gets out and starts looking around expectedly. A barren white room surrounds her and there is a sign next to a chute leading down to the street that says:

"Congratulations! You are our five billionth visitor. There are no men on this floor. This floor exists only in your imagination. Please take this chute down to the street level and turn right to visit the 'PERFECT OUTFIT' store or turn left to shop at our 'PERFECT SHOES' store. Have a nice day!"

THE TEST

A young southern boy was drowned while swimming in a creek. Saint Peter met him at the heavenly gates. Saint Peter explained that because the boy was still young, he had not yet earned a place in heaven. He would be given a chance though, to get in, by taking a short test.

The boy said he would do his best, but hoped it wasn't too hard, because book learning wasn't his strong suit.

There are just three questions said Saint Peter and we adjust them for your age. Answer them correctly and you will spend eternity in heaven. The first is,

"How many days of the week start with the letter 't'?"

The boy thought for a bit before answering,

"Two -today and tomorrow."

Saint Peter was surprised by the answer but, even though it wasn't what he expected, it was correct.

"How about this one? How many seconds are there in a year?"

This was a much tougher question and the boy took some time before delivering his answer.
"Twelve. JAN2cd, Feb2cd, march2cd, april2cd............"

Saint Peter shook his silver-bearded head. Again, it wasn't what was expected, but the boy did have a point.

"Okay," said Saint Peter, "I'm giving you credit for that one as well. Answer this last question right and you will join us in heaven.

"What is God's first name?"

Without much thought, the young boy answered,

"Harold is God's first name."

Taken aback, Saint Peter asks the boy why he thought God's first name is 'Harold'?

"Gosh, everybody knows that. Its in the prayer."

"And which prayer is that?"

"The Lord's Prayer of course..."

"Our Father who art in heaven, Harold be thy name."

THE DUCKS

Three single women friends died together in an auto accident while they were on their way to church. A lovely angel whisked them from their bodies and escorted them to the gates of heaven. Waiting for them was Jesus.

"Welcome to heaven" he said as the Pearly gates opened wide before them. Stepping inside, they gazed in wonder at the infinite beauty that surrounded them. The only puzzlement was the thousands of ducks that wandered everywhere. Jesus explained that the many ducks were much loved by God himself, and that the only rule in heaven was,

"Don't step on the ducks."

The three friends waved good-bye to Jesus and set off to explore the many raptures of their new home. The trees seemed lit by a fury of fall colors all of the time, beautiful waterfalls flowed endlessly into dazzling gardens and loving people smiled on them as they passed.

Then, the first friend got lost looking up at the Auroras in the sky and stepped on a small duck. A loud thunder shook heaven and Jesus reappeared with the ugliest man they had ever seen. Jesus took the wrist of the first friend and with a rough metal shackle, attached her to the arm of the ugly gnome-like man.

"Your punishment for stepping on one of God's ducks is to spend eternity chained to this afflicted man."

The two remaining friends looked on in horror as the ugly creature hauled their friend into a cave in the nearby hill. Jesus again disappeared leaving the two women with their thoughts.

Sadness for their friend must have interfered with their awareness though, - as after barely ten more steps, the second friend also stepped on a duck!

With another crack of thunder, Jesus was back. This time he had an even more hideous man with him who drooled lasciviously as he was manacled to the wrist of the second woman. The last woman watched as the loathsome creature disappeared dragging her friend behind him.

Quite shaken by these experiences, the last woman moved to a part of heaven where there were no ducks to step upon. It was still beautiful but it wasn't near the lovely lake where the ducks seemed to live.

Several months went by without incident. Even in this part of heaven, the woman was careful before taking any steps. Heaven was beautiful and the people friendly but the woman was feeling a little lonely and missed her two friends.

Jesus seemed to be sensing her need for companionship as he appeared before her the next day. With Jesus was the most handsome man the woman had ever seen -tall, muscular with beautiful eyes and a soft smile. Taking the woman's hand, Jesus ceremoniously placed it in the hand of the attractive stranger and bound the two wrists together with a golden cord.

As Jesus left them the woman looked into her new partner's eyes and gratefully said aloud,

"I am so grateful for your company. I'm not sure what I have done to deserve such a wonderful companion."

To this the attractive stranger replied,

"I don't know about you lady, but I stepped on a duck!"

TAKING IT WITH YOU

A wealthy man was near death but was unwilling to leave the massive riches he had earned and still not spent. So, he began to fervently pray that he be allowed to take some of his riches with him into the afterlife.

The man's guardian angel heard the man's prayers and decided to intervene with God on the rich man's behalf. Finding God in a benevolent mood, the angel explained that the rich man had lived a good life and, though still erroneously attached to his material wealth, it would be a great comfort and a generous thing to allow the man to bring some things with him.

God considered the angel's request and decided to grant permission for the man to bring with him one trunk full of those things that mattered to him most.

That night as the rich man slept, the angel appeared to him and conveyed an image of God's willingness to permit the man one trunk full of his most cherished possessions.

The rich man woke the next morning with his body racked with pain but with the memory of the angel's promise still in place. Sensing his own imminent demise, he hurriedly phoned his bank and ordered a trunk full of gold bars be delivered to him that same day.

The rich man breathed his last breath just as the trunk arrived. Tugging the trunk behind him, the rich man entered heaven's gate.

Word that some material reminders of the world had been brought into heaven soon spread. Other souls and angels gathered to welcome the rich man. All wanted to see what was in the trunk.

Great anticipation was felt as the rich man unlocked the trunk and displayed that which was too important to be left behind.

A shocked gasp was heard from the heavenly crowd as the glistening gold bars were revealed. And then the voice of one of the angels,

"He brought pavement?"

HEAVENLY TRASH

An Italian priest, A German minister and a Chinese Zen master arrived in heaven at the same time. God appeared and told the three that they may enter the gates of heaven as soon as they learned to work together and move a huge pile of trash away from the gate.

After God leaves, the Italian Priest volunteers to be in charge of shoveling, The German minister offers to do any sweeping up after the pile is moved and together they tell the Chinaman that all he has to do is take care of getting any supplies they need.

God returns the next day and is very angry. The pile of trash is still sitting in front of heaven's gate. Avoiding God's angry gaze, the Italian priest stutters an apology.

"I so sorry. I no hav-a-no shovel. The Chinese fella was supposed to be in charge of the supplies and he has-as-a disappeared. I could no find-a him nowhere."

The German minister agreed.

"Ach! Dat Chinese fellow No get me zat broom iter."

God is really ticked off now and storms around the trash pile looking for the Chinese Zen master.

Just as he turns the corner, a pile of trash erupts in front of him and the Chinese guy pops out yelling,

"Supplies!"

FLOODS

Harry had survived the 2005 flooding of New Orleans and loved to tell people about his travails during the flood and how he was stranded on a rooftop for three days afterwards. He told his story over and over endlessly until a year later when he was killed in an auto accident.

Harry had lived a good life and went to heaven. Though no longer in body, he still loved to tell about his narrow escape from the flood. One day Jesus came by as Harry had cornered another soul and was again going on tediously about his flood experiences. With compassion, Jesus interrupted his story by placing a hand on both men's shoulders and saying,

"Harry, I'm happy you have finally met our other old friend here - Harry this is <u>Noah</u>."

HEN PECKED

At the gates of heaven, Jesus was speaking to a group of recently arrived male souls.

"All of you men who were the bosses in your homes while on Earth please step to the right."

"All of you men who were subservient to your wives step to your left.

A line quickly formed on the left leaving only one frail looking little man standing by himself to the right.
Jesus looked at the small man and asked'

"What makes you feel you should be on that side?'

The man replied in a timid voice,

"Because that's where my wife told me to stand."

PILOTS

An airline pilot crashed his plane and was taken by the angels to the gates of heaven. There he was asked by Jesus about his life on Earth,

"Did you live a good life?"

"Yes, I think so."

"Did you ever have sex?"

"Yes."

"When was the last time?"

"Oh, about 1958."

"That long ago?"

"I think so. Let me check my watch. Yep, its about 2256 now."

THE ENGINEER

An Engineer dies and arrives at Heaven's gate. An angel at the gate tells him that because he was an engineer, he is at the wrong place. Shaking his head the poor man takes himself down to the gates of hell where he gains immediate entry.

It doesn't take long before the horrible conditions in hell bother the engineer and he starts making some improvements. Using the limited materials in hell, he is able to make a simple air conditioner, build a fountain and add some landscaping.

Then one day God came to pay an unexpected visit to Satan. Looking around at the bubbling fountain, the new flower gardens and feeling the cool air flowing, God asked how this was possible.

Satan laughed and told God that with the help of the engineer, they were thinking of making even more lavish improvements.

God looked startled as he replied,

"An engineer! There must have been a mistake. We don't send engineers to hell. He should not be here. You must send him back."

Satan just sneered and said,

"Forget it! I like having an engineer and he's staying."

God says,

"If you don't sent him back immediately - I'll sue you!"

Satan laughs again and replies,

"And just where are you going to find a *lawyer*!"

THE LOST SON

Jesus was at the gates of Heaven sorting out all the recently-deceased souls. In front of him was a list of all the questions he would ask each one about their family, their lives and some of their deeds on Earth to decide whether they were ready for Heaven or needed to reincarnate into another Earth form.

The day was almost done and Jesus had processed many thousands of souls and directed them on their way. It was just about the time Jesus was due to be relieved by St. Peter that a withered old male soul appeared before him. Jesus looked closely at the old, wrinkled man and asked,

"What job did you have on Earth?"

143

"I was a carpenter."

"Did you have a family?"

"Yes, a wife and a son. But I lost my son."

Jesus looked closely at the man.

"You lost your son? Tell me about him."

"Well the last thing I remember were the holes in his hands and feet."

A gulp rose in Jesus' throat as he uttered the unspoken question,

"Father?"

The old man had a lump in his throat as well as he answered,

"Pinocchio?"

FROZEN

Two women have just arrived at the gates of Heaven. One asks the other how she had died?
She explains, "I froze to death."
The second comments, "How awful!"

"Oh, it wasn't that bad. After I stopped resisting all the shaking from the cold, I was able to fall peacefully asleep and never woke up. And how did you die?"

"I died of a massive stroke. I thought my husband might be cheating on me so, I came home early from work. But, I found him just sitting there in front of the TV by himself. I was still sure something was wrong though and I raced up the stairs to the bedroom and looked under the bed and in the closets. Then I went up into the attic, looked there, and was on my way down to the basement when I felt a pain in my head, tripped on a stair and collapsed from a stroke."

The first woman comforted the woman and replied,

"Honey, its too bad you didn't look in the kitchen freezer first. We'd both still be alive."

FIDELITY

A car carrying three married ministers on their way home from a church conference was destroyed in a terrible accident.

All three men arrived together at heaven's gate. Saint Peter took the first man aside and asked him how many times he had cheated on his wife during their lives together. The minister proudly answered,

"None."

Saint Peter handed the man the keys to a brand new Cadillac to drive around with in heaven. Then Saint Peter turns to the next man and asks him the same question. The minister responds with a bit of guilt,

"Just once."

Saint Peter hands this man the keys to a golf cart to drive around in heaven. Then he turns his attention to the third man who is shifting nervously and asks the question again. The minister answers honestly,

"About a dozen times."

Saint Peter pierces the minister with a fierce look and hands him a broken down old bicycle for his transport in heaven.

The man with the bicycle tries to get it working and begins pumping away at the pedals to get through the gate before anyone changes their mind.

Once inside the gate, the minister on the bike passes the minister in the Cadillac. The car was sitting motionless on the side of the road and the man was inside sobbing his eyes out. The minister on the bike stopped to ask what was the matter. All the minister in the Cadillac could say was,

"I just passed my wife on the road and.... She was walking..."

OCCUPATIONS

An Angel arrives at heaven's gate with the souls of three men. St. Peter is at the gate and tells the men that they will be granted entry to heaven but first he must ask them a few questions to find out what part of heaven they might like best. St. Peter asks the first man,

"How much money did you earn on Earth this past year?"

"Eight hundred thousand dollars."

"Very good. You must have been in real estate. Take the first door to your right."

He then asks the second man the same question. The man answers,

"Fifty thousand dollars."

"Very good. You must have been a minister. Take the second door on your left."

The third man is fidgeting a bit and answers before even being asked,

"I made nine thousand dollars last year."

"That's wonderful," says St. Peter, "and what plays would I have seen you in?"

GOLFING

Tiger Woods dies and goes to Heaven where Jesus meets him. Jesus opens a file showing him what a wonderful life he has lived on Earth with only one very small exception. Tiger asks,

"And what was that?'

Jesus show him the file and there it is.... the use of the Lord's name in vain. Tiger looks at the entry and notes the date. He turns to Jesus to explain,

"I remember now. I was playing in my first major tournament and I was having a great day. I was ahead of the pack and only needed a four on the final hole to win. I teed off and I must have pulled it because it almost sank into the water hazard. But I kept my control and didn't say anything.
I rescued the shot with a long wood shot that landed on the green before it rolled back into a sand trap. I kept my temper as the ball was rolling backwards off that green and into that bunker. I took my time and blasted a wedge shot out of the sand and the ball hit the pin and rolled to within six inches of the cup.
I only needed this little putt to win so, I measured all the possible dips in the green, took a deep breath and....."

"Don't tell me," said Jesus smacking himself on the side of the head, "you missed that damn putt!"

CHALK

Reverends Jim and Jack were good friends who passed away in a car wreck together. Reverend Jim wakes to find himself in heaven where Jesus greets him and hands him an enormous piece of chalk. He asks,

"What's this chalk for Jesus?"

Jesus explains that the first thing everyone does in heaven is to write down all of there shortcomings while on the Earthly plane. He then points to an enormous chalkboard stretching up into the sky with tall ladders reaching upward.

Reverend Jim takes his hugely thick five foot long piece of chalk and starts to climb the nearest ladder. On his way up he notices his friend Reverend Jack on a nearby ladder. He's about to yell a greeting to his friend when he notices that Jack is holding only a small finger-sized piece of chalk.

Reverend Jim starts to reflect ruefully that he indeed would need all of his own chalk to finish his list and how lucky he has been to have such a loyal and goodly friend as Jack. His thoughts are interrupted as he hears Reverend Jack yelling to him,

"Hello Jim, how are you doing?"

Reverend Jim self-consciously tries to tuck his enormous piece of chalk behind him as he replies,

"Fine Jack. Meet you at the top?"

"Nope not now. I'm on my way down for some more of that chalk!"

JESUS

LOOKING FOR JESUS

An old wino is stumbling along the riverbank after a hard night of drinking. He encounters a large group of Baptists dressed in billowing white robes standing in the river. The wino drifts over and stands next to the guy who seems in charge. Suddenly he is being asked,

"And you Sir, are you ready to find Jesus?"

The wino looks back with bleary eyes and mumbles, "Sure am."

The large burly minister next to him grabs the wino by the seat of his pants and the scruff of his neck and plunges the old drunk beneath the water. The wino comes up sputtering water from his mouth and is asked,

"Have you found Jesus?"

"No I haven't."

And the minister pushes him back under with both hands on his head. The wino reemerges looking like a drowned cat. He is asked,

"Have you found Jesus?"

The soaked wino merely shakes his head. The minister grabs him and holds him under water for a full minute. The wino comes up with his eyes popping out of his head and almost sober now. He is asked one more time,

Have you found Jesus?"

This time he answers,

"Are... are you sure this is where he fell in?"

THE CARPENTER AND THE CABINET MAKERS

Many Christian historians find it odd that Jesus, who was a carpenter, chose so many fisherman to be his apostles instead of individuals more closely related like - cabinet makers. That was, until it was explained to them that Jesus would have been loathe to say,

"Drop your drawers and follow me".

JERUSALEM

Jesus walks into a small innkeeper's establishment in Jerusalem, throws three nails down on the front counter and asks,

"Can you put me up for the night?"

JESUS AND ELVIS

Jesus said, "Love thy neighbor".
Elvis sang, "Don't be cruel".

Jesus was the Lord's shepherd.
Elvis dated Cybil Shepherd.

Jesus was part of the divine trinity.
Elvis's first band was a trio.

Jesus said, "If any man thirsth, let him come to me and drinkith."
Elvis said, "Drinks on me".

Jesus wore white robes.
Elvis wore a white jump suit.

Jesus lives in a state of grace.
Elvis lived in Graceland.

Jesus was resurrected.
Elvis had a famous comeback tour.

HELL

GATE TO HELL

A geological expedition that had been drilling deep into the Earth found a strange old wooden door barring their path. It had burnt red inscriptions on its surface and archaeological experts were brought in to decipher the significance of their find.

A specialist in ancient languages was able to translate most of the words on the door as,

"ABANDON HOPES ALL YE WHO ENTER HERE. THE FIRES OF HELL AWAIT THEE"

The scientists thought it was some kind of prank but an analysis of the door showed that it was indeed very ancient. To be on the safe side, it was decided that a religious expedition should be sent to investigate what lay beyond the door.

The Pope was contacted and he agreed to send a Catholic team of investigators into the hole behind the gate for a fee of one million dollars, all of which the church would keep at the Vatican.

A Jewish team was contacted and they said they would make the expedition but they would have to charge two million dollars. One million for their synagogue and one million to reimburse the religious team.

A Protestant minister was asked about the services of his church's Christian team and he said they would take care of it for a charge of three million dollars.

The administrator of the project questioned the minister about his need for so much money.

"Its simple," said the minister, "one million for the church, one million for me for setting it up and ... one million to pay the Catholic team to go."

WHICH HELL

A crooked politician died after a lengthy illness. At the gates of hell, he is asked by the devil at the gate whether he would prefer to enter democratic hell or communist hell.

Having been raised in America, the politician is about to say democratic hell, but asks the devil first how they might be different. The devil explains that if he is uncertain, he may visit both before deciding.

The politician decides to visit both. At the gates to democratic hell he is met by Donald trump. The politician asks Trump about democratic hell.

Trump answers that in democratic hell they are cut all over by demons with knives, salt poured in the wounds, tossed into boiling oil and then ripped apart by hungry animals. Then they are given another body and the torture begins all over again.

The politician is shaken by the horror of this 'democratic' eternity. In desperation, he walks over to the gate marked communist hell.

Outside this gate Joe Stalin meets him. The evil communist dictator looks terrible. The politician asks with a quavering voice,

"What's it like in there in communist hell?"

Stalin's bruised; bleeding figure looks up mournfully and answers,

"It's terrible. They slice you with knives, salt the wounds and boil you in oil before they let the animals attack what's left. And then it starts all over again"

"But... But that sounds just like democratic hell!"

"True," says Stalin, "but here we sometimes don't have oil, and sometimes we don't have enough knives."

GOOD THINGS ABOUT HELL

There is plenty of legal help available for wrongful death lawsuits.

There are spacious smoking sections.

It's a 'dry' heat.

The boiling vats of brimstone have been switched to a healthier low-fat canola oil.

Its fun to watch Satan trying to torture sado-masochists.

The free daily prostate checks and 'welcome O.J.' T-shirts.

Short Stuff

Our minister is over eighty years old and doesn't need glasses.
He drinks straight from the bottle.

The young minister's nose was broken in three places. The church's
board chairman said that he hoped the young man would learn from his
experience - and stay out of those three places.

What do you get if you cross an angel and a skunk?
Something that stinks to High Heaven.

The minister went to a psychiatrist to consult with him about his inferiority
complex. The doctor told him he should not consider it to be a problem
because ... he really was inferior.

The doctor told our ailing minister that he should be able to continue living
a completely normal life. As long as he didn't try to enjoy it!

An atheist is someone with no <u>invisible</u> means of support.

The pretty young girl was overheard praying:

"Dear Lord, I ask nothing for myself. But could you bring my poor
suffering mother a rich, handsome young son-in-law?"

The minister's wife got her birth control pills mixed up with her Nutrasweet
tablets.
She and the minister now have the sweetest baby you have ever seen.

Bumper Sticker: OUR MINISTER USED TO BE INDECISIVE.
                         NOW HE'S NOT SO SURE

Acupuncture is used for many health issues in Asia. But, we know of a
medically trained missionary there who practices traditional surgery.
He calls it 'Chinese Take Out'.

Bumper Sticker: 'Be Modest and be Proud of it'

An optimistic Christian minister was asked if there was anything good he could say about egotistical people? He thought about it a moment before replying,
"At least they don't gossip a lot about <u>other</u> people."

The picky lady minister went into an expensive hair salon for a haircut.
When the stylist was done she asked the minister if she was satisfied?
The minister looked at it in the mirror and replied,
"Not really. Couldn't you just make it a little <u>longer</u> in back?"

The lady minister at a church in the Ozarks announced that there would be a new beauty contest at the next church social.
But it was canceled after the first year when NOBODY won.

The same lady minister complained that the photographer was not taking her picture from her 'best side'. He explained that he couldn't because –
 She was sitting on it.

A well-known TV evangelist claimed- that he would be using the devotee's donations to build a ten thousand story building in God's name. It turned out to be the truth.... but he hadn't mentioned it was a library.

One of the hardest stories to believe in the Old Testament is the one about Noah.
Could there really only have been two asses on that Ark?

An enlightened minister had been having trouble keeping his church full during the hot summer months. As the heat rose, more and more members were finding reasons to leave the service early. In the church bulletin the minister announced he would be dividing his sermons to serve all factions of the church. The first half of the sermon would be to help all the sinners in the congregation. The second half of the sermon would be to honor those with clear consciences.
No one left early that Sunday.

The new minister was so short of personality and boring that the other ministers used to take him with them when - they wanted to be alone

A new congregant asked the minister about the average Sunday donation?
"Its about twenty dollars."
"Wow," said the new member handing over a twenty, "This must be a very rich church."
"Not really," replied the minister. "Yours is the first average donation in quite a while."

Baptists commit sins just like all other Christians. It's just that their religion forbids them from enjoying them.

One of the ladies at the church complained that she had nothing to do.
So, the minister signed her up for a bridge club.
She jumps next Thursday.

The minister asked the young man if he thought his fiancée was loyal to him? He replied,
"I don't think it. I know!"
The minister replied,
"I don't think you know either."

Then there was the Christian cannibal who liked to stop at a jungle mission church that was 'dedicated to serving mankind'.

A highway patrolman stopped a lady minister on her way to church. He told her that his radar gun said she was going over a hundred miles an hour.
She explained that there must be a mistake as it was physically impossible for that to be true.
"How so, " asked the officer?
She pointed at her watch and explained there was no way she could have been driving for a whole hour.

Reverend Lucy told her friend that she had just confronted her beau and told him that she didn't want to see him anymore. Her friend exclaimed,
"Wow, how did he react?"
"He turned off the light."

Church Dictionary: Flex-atarian - a vegetarian with occasional lapses.

The little cafe next to the bible college advertised a
'Thank God its Monday' happy hour.

Atheists now have a phone number to call when they are in distress. It's a lot like
Dial a Prayer, except that when <u>it</u> rings ... no one picks up.

Some people think the new minister has a big head.
Others say he is just a lame brain.
I don't repeat any of that gossip.
I just tell people that he likes to wear orthopedic hats.

Reverend Beatrice told her old friend Reverend Alice that,
"I've been in France for over a week and I haven't been to the Louvre yet."
Rev. Alice remarked, "Here, try some prunes."

The young Amish girl angrily accused the gawky boy next to her at church,
"Are you looking at my ankles?"
"No," he replied. "I'm above that."

Bumper Sticker:
PLEASE PRACTICE MODERATION - BUT NOT TO EXCESS.

The minister won a large amount of money playing the state lottery. He didn't want to tell his wife about the money so he decided to hide it in the house. He looked and looked for a safe place to hide the money and finally found a secure one ... under the vacuum cleaner.

A Lutheran minister we know refused to say that he was a 'bad dancer'.
But, he <u>did</u> admit that his dancing could be considered 'overly Caucasian'.

"Reverend, what happened between you and that pretty red-headed gypsy girl you dated?"
"I told her she had to take me or leave me."
"Wow. What did she do?"
"BOTH."

A lady minister was visiting the Southwest for the first time and was shown a fig tree by a friend. She replied,
"Are you sure that's really a fig tree like - in Adam & Eve in the Bible?'
"Yes," her friend said, then asked, "Haven't you ever seen a fig tree before Reverend?"
"Well, no. I guess that's what is bothering me - I always thought the leaves would be a bit BIGGER."

An American minister was visiting Spain. He had to use the bathroom
desperately but couldn't remember the Spanish word for bathroom.
The last we heard, he was still rushing down the road asking directions
to - the 'Juan'.

Reverend Clem decided to send a jigsaw picture of himself to a woman he
met on the internet.
He wanted her to get used to seeing his face ... GRADUALLY.

A cannibal rushed up to the jungle mission and asked if he was too late for
supper?
Yes, he was told, because everybody's already eaten.

A young lady was asked by her friend,
"Elaine, weren't you engaged to marry that promising young minister?"
"Promising, yes. But - he didn't keep his promises."

If a man is walking in the woods expressing himself and no woman hears
him, is he still wrong?

A missionary was telling the church audience how he had come across a
tribe of wild women living in the jungle - and not one of them had a tongue.
"Wow. How did they speak?"
"They didn't. That's what made them so wild."

The minister and his new wife were considered to be the perfect couple.
They had met in college where he had honed his public speaking skills and
she had been a theater major. Now he spoke to large church audiences and
she could ACT LIKE SHE WAS LISTENING.

"Minister, minister.... I think I need your help."
"What can I do for you?"
"I keep having this awful dream that I am a dog."
"Well, why don't you just calm down, take a seat and we'll talk about it."
"I can't."
"Why not?"
"I'm not allowed on the furniture."

The church elder and his wife got a divorce because of religious differences.
He thought he was God ... and she didn't.

A certain minister liked to hang mistletoe above the collection plate at his church. It was, he stated,
"For those who wanted to kiss their money good-bye!"

After a particularly long sermon in the congregation's brand new church, a grumpy old deacon was asked about the acoustics in the building.
"Terrible,' he replied, "I could hear every word the minister said".

The minister argued that the members of his congregation were <u>not</u> cheap. It was just that they ... had low pockets and short arms.

Old Proverb:
 If one man callith thee a donkey, pay him no heed.
 If more than one man callith thee a donkey, getteth thee a saddle.

An excited new minister called 911 and explained that his church was on fire. The fire department operator asked,
"How do we get to your church?"
The new minister replied,
"Don't you have any of those red trucks with the hoses anymore?"

There was a minister who was so frugal that he always sharpened his pencils over the fireplace so that he wouldn't waste any WOOD.

A passenger plane crashed into a cemetery in the Ozarks. The local minister directing the response team has been said to have already recovered over three thousand bodies.

The minister loved to play golf every Sunday afternoon. This particular Sunday he was having a difficult day and was loosing his calm demeanor. Finally, he looked over at his caddie and complained that,
"You must be the worst caddie in the world."
To which his caddie replied,
"No. That would be <u>too</u> much of a coincidence."

A ministerial student was comforting a fellow student who had been badly beaten up.
He told his friend,
"You shouldn't have told that big guy that his girlfriend was ugly."
"I didn't. I just asked if she was allowed on the furniture?"

A local church was having a church picnic. As it got dark a little boy came up to the minister and asked if there were such things as vampires? The darkly robed minister replied that he didn't know for sure but... that the boy had better drink his soup before it clotted.

"Reverend, reverend ... I'm on a new diet. Do you think grapefruit are healthy?"
"Well, I don't know, but I've never heard one complain."

An astronaut took a Bible with him on his trip into space. When he got back he reported that he just hadn't been able to 'put it down'.

The town's different religious denominations decided to hold a large ecumenical conference at a nudist camp. Why?
Because they thought it would be a good way to 'air their differences'.

The minister's new wife asked him to please make up some fresh juice and toast and told him "breakfast would soon be ready".
The minister squeezed the juice, toasted some bread and asked,
"What are we having for breakfast Darling?"
The answer: "Toast and Juice."

The minister's younger brother offered to baby-sit for the weekend. He said he would take the children to the zoo. When the minister and his wife got home they asked the kids how they had enjoyed the zoo? The oldest boy explained,
"We loved it! The best part was when everyone got up and cheered as the animals came romping home to the finish line."

The ministerial student was seen dating some much older women.
When asked why, he replied,
"Because they can't slap as hard".

Mary and Joseph rode to Bethlehem on the back of their faithful donkey. What no one today knows is that - the donkey had an IQ of over a hundred and sixty.
After Jesus was born, Joseph sold the donkey to a passing nomad. When asked why he had parted with this loyal, intelligent animal, he replied,
"I guess no one really likes a smart ass."

Bumper Sticker: TWO CAN LIVE AS CHEAPLY AS ONE
                 BUT ONLY FOR HALF AS LONG

The vain young minister was starting to lose his hair. It was falling out on his pillow every night. He had a consult with a physician and asked, "Doctor, do you have anything to keep my hair in?"
The physician shrugged and handed him an empty box.

A distraught Sunday School teacher came rushing up to the minister and told him that Little Billy had swallowed his ball point pen. The minister said he would be there in a minute. Then he asked what they had already done about it?
"We're letting him use his pencil."

The minister raised his hands to Heaven in the middle of his sermon and proclaimed loudly,
"Without you Lord, we are but dust."
Little Lucy in the back row leaned over to her mother and asked,
"Mommy, what is butt dust?"

A young missionary had just been liberated after ten years spent in a religious cult.
The church elders asked him why he hadn't tried to escape sooner?
He replied,
"They told me I was gullible. And, I believed them."

A professed bigamist was asked to leave the church because he couldn't be allowed to 'have his Kate and Edith too.'

A German minister and his family had just moved to Texas and were going out to eat at an American restaurant for the first time. In the middle of the meal, the minister's son asked,
"Father, I think there is something wrong with these Buffalo wings."
"Why do you say that Son?"
"They taste like chicken."

"Our new minister has 'pedestrian' eyes."
"What do you mean 'pedestrian' eyes?'
"I mean they look both ways before they cross."

Prison Chaplain to condemned man:
"I will allow you ten minutes of grace before they execute you."
Prisoner's reply:
"That's not very much time Reverend. But bring her in."

A missionary just back from the jungles of Africa was asked,
"How did you manage to avoid all those diseases caused by biting insects?"
"I didn't bite any."

Things a new minister shouldn't say at a Baptism:
"What a cute baby. Who's the father?"

The bishop made Arnold Palmer a priest so that he could compete for the
Catholic team at the annual Ecumenical Golf Tournament. The Catholic
team still lost, coming in second to the Protestant team and Reverend Tiger
Woods.

A man was consulting his minister about his guilt for having sexual dreams.
The minister explained he shouldn't feel guilty as long as the dreams were
only erotic and not perverse. The man was not certain what this meant and
asked the minister how to tell the difference?
"Well," explained the minister, "if there was just a feather in them, that is
erotic. But if there is a whole chicken - that is perverse."

The dyslexic sinner sold his soul to SANTA.

The minister's wife left him to run away with a tractor salesman. He said
that he couldn't believe it until.... He got the 'John Deere' letter.

"Reverend, my wife needs some counseling for her immaturity."
"Immaturity?'
"Yes, immaturity. Every time I'm taking a bath, she comes in and sinks all
my boats."

"Reverend, I wish I had my wife back."
"Where is she?'
"Last year I got drunk and traded her for a case of beer."
"Tsk! Tsk! So, now you realize you love and miss her?"
"Not really. I'm just thirsty again."

The Bible doesn't mention that Jesus had a dyslexic younger brother. When
the younger brother was asked what he and his family did for a living, he
said they were crapenders.

An Amish elder had a wife who was the worse driver in rural Pennsylvania.
Even their horse had dents.

BUMPER STICKER: " WHEN IN DOUBT, FAITH IT."

Why do Baptists object to fornication?
"Because it violates the Ten Commandments?"
"No. Because it might lead to dancing."

In Africa even the cannibals are going on diets.
They now only eat <u>thin</u> missionaries.

How many Amish does it take to roof a barn?
It depends on how thin you slice them.

The new church secretary was sure that the new minister was a bit too
persnickety when she opened his file cabinet and found them all sub labeled
'Sacred' and 'Top Sacred'.

Our church dictionary says REINTARNATION is coming back in another
life as a hillbilly.

What do you get when you cross a lion and a preacher?
I don't know. But when it speaks, you listen!

The preacher's sermon had been so reverent and heart-felt that the
congregation gave him a kneeling ovation.

An agnostic friend of ours was upset when he came home from a vacation
and found that someone had burned a question mark into his front lawn.

Our minister is so skinny that if we sent his picture to Africa, they would be
sending <u>us</u> food."

The minister was said to be so lazy that in starting a family, he was looking
to marry someone that was already pregnant.

My minister told me that my spiritual path wouldn't amount to much
because I procrastinate all the time. I told him, "You just wait and see."

What do Christians in Africa call the Easter bunny?

Dinner.

What do you call a televangelist preacher who has no hands?

Honest.

What do you call a missionary with only half of a brain?

Gifted.

The lazy minister surprised his wife when he told her he had found a job. She learned later that though he had found it - he hadn't <u>gotten</u> it.

A point to ponder: Have you ever visited the home of a faith healer? And been tempted to look in their medicine cabinet?

An older minister explained that he knew it was time to move from Alaska when he went to take out the garbage on one freezing morning - and it just wouldn't go!

The minister told all of his friends that he 'wore the pants' in his family. But his whole congregation knew that it was his wife who decided 'what kind of pants'.

What goes, 'Clip, Clop,Clip Clop, Bang, Bang, Clippity Clop, Clippity Clop?'
An Amish drive by shooting.

A good test of faith is to be at church during the Sunday collection, look into your wallet and see ONLY hundred dollar bills

The church bulletin announced that because of the large number of baptisms scheduled that day, they would be using the chapel at the North end of the church as well as the one at the South end.
And that the children would be baptized at 'both ends'.

The minister was pleased when one of his congregation said that his last sermon had been,
"A Rolls Royce-like lesson."
Then thinking about it more that night he realized that the two most notable aspects of that particular car were the smooth-running, difficult-to-hear engine and that they seemed to GO ON FOREVER.

The cannibal chief sent his son to the mission school for a Christian education. When the boy graduated with honors, his father asked him if he could still eat people?
"Sure Dad. Only now I have to use a knife and fork."

A little boy at Sunday School asked one of the little girls to go outside with him and play 'Adam and Eve'. She smiled and asked him,
"How do you play Adam and Eve?
He explained,
"First you tempt me. Then I give in."

A masked robber waylaid an older lady minister and searched her for ten minutes looking unsuccessfully for valuables. He was about to put his gun down and give up but asked first,
"Lady, don't you have any money or jewelry?"
"No. But if you keep on searching, I'll write you a check."

The minister received the following thank you letter for his birthday gift to a little girl.
"Dear Reverend Tom: Thank you very much for my birthday gift. I've always wanted a nice new Bible - though not very much."

The cannibal ate his mother-in-law and discovered that she still disagreed with him,

What did the cannibal chief get his wife for Valentine's Day?
A two-pound box of farmer's fannies.

A minister was playing golf for the first time. He took a huge swing at the ball, missed and tore a huge divot out of the grass. He looked at the ball still sitting there, picked up the grass divot and asked his caddie what he should do next? The caddie just looked at the huge divot, shook his head and told the minister,
"Why not just take it home ... to practice on."

The minister complained that his wife said he was a busybody and that he should stay out of other people's business. The other ministers agreed that she shouldn't say things like that and that she should be admonished. Then, the minister added.
"Well, she didn't actually <u>say</u> it. But I <u>did</u> read it in her diary."

God made man <u>before</u> he made woman.
That's because he didn't want any advice on how to make man.

A lady minister from Maine was talking to a minister from Georgia.
"Some of these southern men can be pretty silly sometimes.
Men are all alike."
Her Southern Sister replied,
"Men are all ah like too."

A minister's young daughter returned from the movies looking a bit disheveled.
The minister's wife asked what had happened to her clothing?
"I had to get up and change seats six times."
"Was someone bothering you."
"Yes. Finally."

An unmarried lady minister we know tells everyone she could have married anyone she pleased. I guess she didn't please anyone.

Another lady minister asked her fiancée if he would still love her as much after they were married?
"Sure. I've always been particularly attracted to married women."

Two evangelists are talking. One shares that the Devil had appeared to him in a dream the previous night and offered to make him a congressional chaplain in exchange for his immortal soul. His friend comments,
"That's wonderful. But what's the catch?"

The young missionary wanted to prove his love to his new wife. So, he swam the deepest river, climbed the highest mountain and crossest the widest desert for her. She left him because he was never home.

One minister's wife said to another.
"I got a new set of golf clubs for my husband."
The other responded,
"I wonder how much I can get for mine?"

The hostess told the visiting minister that,
"A storm seems to be on its way – You'd better stay for dinner."
"No," he replied, "I don't think the storm could be that bad!"

The Dean of Students asked the bible student if he had shaved this day?
"Yes Sir."
"Next time stand closer to the razor."

The minister asked a young boy why he had stolen money from the church collection box. The boy answered:

"I wasn't feeling very well Reverend. I thought the change might do me some good."

YOUR SOLE PURPOSE IN LIFE MAY BE TO - SERVE AS A WARNING TO OTHERS.

A minister with too much pride was said to be suffering from his "Altar Ego".

Our minister said that when it comes to giving, many of his flock will stop at nothing.

CHURCH SIGN
The water of salvation is free. But it costs a lot for the 'plumbing'.

THE BIBLE

Heard in Third Grade Bible Study

Moses came down from Mt. Cyanide with ten commandos.

The seventh commandment is thou shalt not admit adultery.

Joshua fought the battle of Geritol.

King Solomon had 300 wives and 700 porcupines.

Jesus was born of Mary in an act of immaculate contraception.

The epistles were the wives of the apostles.

Jesus had twelve opossums.

Christians are limited to one wife. We call it monotony.

Jews throughout history have had problems with unsympathetic genitals.

What kind of coats did Adam and Eve wear?
Bare skin.

Why couldn't they play cards on those long 40 days on Noah's ark?
They were sitting on the deck.

The Leaf

A young girl was flipping through the pages of her family bible at Sunday school. Amongst the pages was a dried up leaf from an old oak tree that had been pressed between the pages.

As she turned to the next page, the leaf fluttered out and landed next to the Sunday school teacher. Looking down, the teacher asked the girl what had fallen.

The little girl thought for a second & said,

"I think it's Adam's suit."

Garden of Eden

God created Adam and placed him in the Garden of Eden. But Adam was sad and God asked what was the matter? Adam said he was lonely and didn't have anyone to talk to. God told him that he this could be easily fixed. God would create a woman. Adam was excited and wanted to know more about this thing called woman.

God explained that woman would be his constant companion, his helpmate. The woman would cook, clean bear and raise his children. She would love him, console him and never nag or disagree with his plans.

Adam couldn't believe his good fortune and thanked God, asking if this great gift would cost him anything. God replied that yes, there would be the cost of an arm and a leg.

To which Adam replied

"And what can I get for a rib?"

Adam and Eve

When Adam's children grew up, they asked their father why they no longer lived in the paradise of Eden. He whispered that their mother had,

'Eaten them out of house and home'.

Trusting Adam

Adam and Eve were living happily together in the Garden of Eden before that awful 'apple' incident. Then one day Eve looked at Adam sitting there with a smile on his face and asked him,

"Adam, do you love me with all your heart?"

"Of course Eve. How silly a question. Who else could there be?"

But Eve didn't trust Adam and set the stage for all that came after by waiting until Adam fell asleep each night and then she snuck over to ... COUNT HIS RIBS.

Grandpa

The white-bearded grandpa is bouncing his three-year-old granddaughter on his lap. She looks up and tells him that they had been learning bible stories in Sunday school. She then asks,

"Were you on Noah's ark Grandpa?"

Grandpa just looks back at her with a smile and tells her that he wasn't. She fixes her eyes on his shaggy face and wants to know,

"Then, how come you didn't drown?'

The First Man

Eve was alone in the Garden of Eden but was not happy. God came to her and asked what was wrong.

"God, this is a beautiful place you have created and I enjoy all the other creatures but I am still lonely for someone to talk to when you aren't here."

"Well Eve, I think I have a solution. I will create a man to keep you company. Man is an aggressive, flawed creature with a huge ego. He'll be bigger and stronger and, though he will listen to you, he will not understand much. He will give you someone to talk to but, are you willing to put up with his problems?"

"Oh yes God! When can you create him?"

"Well, I can probably do it tomorrow, but there is one other condition."

"What's that god?"

"You'll have to let him believe I created him first."

Ambrosia

Our minister was describing an Old Testament character in his sermon. This man had over a hundred wives and he fed them all with ambrosia.
An older man in the back of the congregation stood up suddenly and asked loudly,

"NEVER MIND WHAT HE FED THEM. WHAT DID HE EAT?"

PMS

After a long Sunday sermon describing how the bible speaks to every condition in the human experience, the minister was asked by one of the ladies in private.

"What about PMS? Does the bible say anything about Pre-Menstrual Syndrome?"

The minister replied confidently that though no verse came to him at that moment, he was sure that he could find a bible reference about PMS and would share it with her the following week.

The minister looked diligently through his bible line by line that week and when the woman approached him the following Sunday, he pointed out a particular verse to her and read aloud,

"And Mary rode Joseph's ass all the way to Bethlehem."

PSALMS 129

Pete, one of the widower's in our church picked up a young hitchhiker. The young woman got into his car and while crossing her legs her dress slid up a bit to reveal an ample thigh.

Pete tried not to observe too obviously but after a few miles he reached across the seat and touched the exposed thigh. The young woman looked him in the eyes and said,

"Sir. Please remember Psalms 129!"

Feeling reproached, Pete pulled his hand away. But after a few more miles the woman leaned over to look out her window. The movement exposed even more of her thigh and Pete's hand returned to the thigh. The woman turned around and again proclaimed,

"Sir. Please remember Psalms 129!"

Pete again removed his hand. A few miles more and the young woman asked to be let out at a truck stop. She exited the car with a heavy sigh and Pete noticed her wave as he pulled away. As soon as he got home Pete pulled out his bible and turned to Psalms 129:

"Go forth and seek, further up you will find Glory."

Lot and his Wife

A Christian father was reading from the bible to his young children one evening. He told them about the man named 'Lot' who was warned by God to take his wife and flee from the wicked city of Sodom and Gomorrah. Lot's wife had turned to look back and was turned into a pillar of salt.

The kids looked suitably impressed by the story but the smallest child still wanted to know what happened to the 'flea'.

MARRIAGE AND FAMILY

Marriage

It was said that the minister's wife had made him into a millionaire.
Before marriage, he had been a <u>multi</u>-millionaire.

After meeting his new wife's family, the young minister decided to cut off
his dog's tail.
He just didn't want his new mother-in-law to feel <u>too</u> welcomed at their
house.

The minister's wife began to suspect he was involved with his church
secretary.
The lipstick stains on his collar had been covered with whiteout.

A good wife always forgives her husband when she's wrong.

Asked why she wore her wedding ring on the wrong finger, she replied.
"I married the wrong man."

The minister said he had not spoken to his wife in over a month - he didn't
want to interrupt her.

I married Miss Right but, I didn't know her first name was 'Always".

The minister's fiancée said they couldn't even talk about sex until they
were married.
On their honeymoon she said, 'Okay, now we can talk about it."

A minister told his new young wife that men are like fine wines.
They improve with age.... So she locked him in the cellar.

The minister advised the young wife to take more of an interest in her husband's activities. She did.... she hired a detective.

The preacher's wife walked into the beauty parlor sporting a swollen black eye. Her friends asked how she had gotten it? She replied,
"From my husband."
"But we thought your husband was out of town at a revival meeting."
"So did I."

Memories

A distraught woman sought out the minister for counseling. She was concerned that her aging husband kept waking each morning and asking,

"Where am I Catherine?"

"I see," said the minister. "And you are worried that your husband may be getting Alzheimer's?"
The woman looked a little bit puzzled, before replying,

"Well no. I was just a bit concerned because my name is Margaret."

Family Man

A rural minister took his large family to the state fair. At the sideshow they saw a huge tent with a sign advertising the 'World's Most Valuable Bull'. The barker outside asked the minister if he'd like to come inside and see the amazing animal. The minister replied,

"I'd sure like to see that bull of yours. But so would the rest of my family - and as you can see, with the twelve kids and my wife, we just can't afford it."

The barker looked at the large family and told the minister,

"Just go on and come on in for free. I want that bull of mine to take a look at YOU."

Sex Talk

Our minister was a little concerned when his eight-year-old daughter approacheed him and wanted to know what sex is? He hemmed and hawed a bit and told her about the birds and the bees. She interrupted him and said that all of that may be very interesting, but what is sex? The minister doesn't know how to continue and instead asks her,

"Why do you want to know so badly?"

She answers,

"I guess it doesn't really matter that much but Mommy just told me that supper will be ready in JUST A COUPLE OF SECS."

Daughter's Wedding

The gruff old minister's eldest daughter was finally getting married. The old minister cornered the young man and demanded,

"So, do you really think you are finally ready to support a family?"

The young man retorted,

"No. I'm ready to support your daughter. You and the rest of your family will have to support yourselves."

Bad Acting

The minister's daughter had been acting for some time in community plays but she just didn't have that certain quality that all good actors require. In fact she was so awful playing her part in the church's most recent production of ' The Sound of Music' that when the Nazis arrived looking for any members of the Von Trapp family, several members of the church audience jumped up and shouted,

"She's hiding in the closet."

New Husband

The minister's daughter returns from a journey through Africa. The minister and his wife greet her as she gets off her plane. Next to her is a dark-skinned native with a bone through his nose and feathers in his hair. The girl introduces her new husband to her parents. The minister's wife grabs her head and screams,
"No. No. I said find a rich doctor. A <u>rich</u> doctor!"

Christmas Gift

An older minister is visiting his son and his grandkids for Christmas. It is Christmas morning and the three young boys are excitedly opening the gifts under the tree. They get to their grandfather's gift and they all yell in unison,

"Dad, look what Grandpa got us! Super-soaker water cannons!"

The kids head for the sink to fill their new weapons. The son has a grimace on his face as he turns to the aged minister and says,

"Dad, don't you remember what an awful mess we made out of your house when we got those same kind of water guns as kids?"

The old minister just smiled at his son and replied,

"I do."

The Sinner

Reverend Rightly was listening to one of the ladies from his parish.

'Reverend, my husband Willy comes home from work later and later every night. My friends say they have seen him all over town drinking in pubs, chasing women and gambling."

"That's terrible! Your husband is a miserable sinner."

"Well that's the problem Reverend. Willy may indeed be a sinner. But miserable, no. He seems to be having the time of his life."

The Murderer

The old Anglican bishop lived alone in retirement in the countryside. His only son, Reggie had lived with the bishop but had been recently taken away to prison for murdering his employer. The disheartened bishop decided to put in a small garden to bring some color and cheer to his solitary life.

But as he tried to dig, he found the ground too hard and full of rocks to deal with in his frail condition. The old man wrote to his son in prison:

"Dear Reggie,
I miss you so much. I tried to put in a flower garden today to remind me of your cheerful company. Alas, the ground is too hard and I will have to remember you in other ways.

Love Dad."

A few days later he received a return note from his son.

"Dear Dad,
Please don't dig in the backyard! The other bodies are buried there!

Love Reggie."

That night at midnight, the prison warden, the coroner and the police arrived and without even speaking to the old bishop, they pushed past him and proceeded into the back yard with picks and shovels. Four hours later they muttered a brief apology on their way out.

The next day the bishop received a second letter from his son.

"Dear Dad,
Sorry I couldn't help you with the garden, but this was the best I could do under the circumstances. I hope you enjoy putting in the flowers.

Love Reggie."

Dinner Blessing

A country minister took his family into the city for a holiday meal. They sat down and bowed their heads to bless the meal. Some loud teenagers at a nearby table snickered and yelled out,

"Hey farmer-man. Does everyone have to do that where you come from?"

"No," replied the minister. "The pigs certainly don't."

175

Marital Discord

The minister had struggled to make his marriage work. But after counseling and much prayer he told his young wife,

"Our marriage is not working. We can't seem to agree on anything. I know it's only been seven months but I think we need to get a divorce."

His wife looked at him and stridently replied,

"Eight months. It's been eight months!"

Breakfast with Jesus

A Christian mother was preparing breakfast for her two sons. The boys started to argue about who should get the first waffle. The mother realized this would be a good opportunity to teach the boys about her faith and said...

"If Jesus was sitting here, he would say, 'let my brother have the first pancake and I will wait.'"

The older of the two boys nodded his head in understanding and looked at his younger brother stating,

"Brian, it's your turn to be Jesus."

Grandchildren

In the small local church it was noticed when a sweet white-haired grandmother placed twice her usual offering into the weekly collection basket.

The minister sought the woman out later and thanked her for her generosity. He couldn't help asking the reason for it. She answered with a smile,

"It is because my grandchildren are finally coming to visit me - and I'm so grateful."

Two weeks later the same grandmother is noticed increasing her offering by a factor of four. Again, the minister seeks her out for an explanation.

"They just left."

Microphone

An evangelical preacher was on stage for the weekend revival meeting. He wore a small microphone at his throat wired to a long extension cord to give him freedom of movement across the stage.

The revival started and the preacher was lifting his hands to heaven, stomping back and forth across the stage and swinging the cord around with him as he moved.

A little girl in the first row had been to the circus the previous weekend and now was here with her family for her first revival meeting. She watched the preacher's performance quietly with rapt attention. At the intermission, her mother asked what she thought of the revival so far?

She answered with a slight quiver in her voice,

"Mommy? Will he hurt us if he gets loose?"

Meditation

Two ministers were walking down the street.
One stops and asks the other how he is doing. He answers,

"Fine, and how are you?"

"I'm good, thanks."

"And how is your family? Is your eldest son still unemployed?"

"Yes, he hasn't been able to find anything just yet, but he is meditating a lot in the meantime."

"Meditating, what's that?"

"I don't know - but it sure beats him sitting around doing nothing!"

Giggling

Little Reggie was obstinate and irreverent. His sister told him he had to stop giggling and fooling around during the church service. He responded with,

 "Who's going to make me?"

His sister pointed to the adults standing at he back of the church and whispered, "The 'hushers'".

Menopause

One of the men in the congregation took the minister aside and asked,

"Reverend, my wife is about to start menopause. Is there anything I need to do?"

The minister shook his head silently, and then asked the man if he was any good with construction tools?

"Why yes," replied the man. "I did some building when I was younger. "

"Good," answered the minister. "My advice is to take those tools out and finish the room you started up in your attic. Then when you're finished you'll at least have a place to live for a while."

Wine in the Car

Suzy was driving home from her relative's house in another state. As she got nearer to home she saw her elderly minister walking on the side of the road. The weather was getting colder so she stopped and offered the minister a ride back to her house.

The minister accepted the offer and plunked her elderly body down in the front seat next to Suzy. After exchanging a few pleasantries the old minister turned and noticed a large box on the back seat of the car. She asked Suzy what was in it?

Suzy was a bit flustered at the question but answered honestly.

"It's a case of wine."

The old minister's nose turned up in distaste so, Suzy added,

"I got it for my husband."

The old minister replied with the quiet wisdom of her many years,

"Good trade!"

SCREWING IN A LIGHT BULB

How many does it take to Screw in a Light bulb?

Catholics - none, they prefer candles.

Muslims - none. Allah has predestined when the lights will go on and off.

Evangelicals - one, and easily, because their hands are in the air already.

Mormons - Eight. one man to change the bulb and seven wives to tell him how to do it.
]
Jehovah witnesses - fifty. One to change it and forty nine to pray against the forces of the dark.

Baptists - Changgggge?????

Amish - 'What's a light bulb?'

Youth ministers - We don't know - they aren't around long enough.

Atheists - one, but they are still in darkness.

Zen Buddhists - one to change it, one not to change it.

Jewish Rabbis - Five. One to call a handyman to screw the bulb in and four to feel guilty about spending the money.

Heterosexual Catholic Priests - Both of them.

Women Ministers - Two. One to pour the diet coke and one to call the handyman.

Fundamentalist Christians - Sorry, the Bible doesn't mention light bulbs.

How to know when you've slipped into New Age Spirituality?

Do you have a sweet, low-maintenance animal spirit guide?

Do you monitor the color of your aura?

Do you spend most of your day cleansing your chakras?

Are you psychically connected to your dead relatives and follow their advice?

Do you keep a forked-stick in your garage in case a new neighbor needs to drill a well?

Do you carry on entertaining conversations with your plants?

Do you have a pet psychic's number on your phone's speed dial?

Have you ever stayed home solely because Mercury was in retrograde?

Have you ever been hit by a car and told the cop, "I manifested this"?

Do you like your spirit guides better than your real friends?

Do you have a tantric sex manual on your coffee table?

Thanks to aromatherapy, does your house smell better than you do?

Do you have kids with names like Tree, Whisper or Celery?

Do you pray for the souls of the vegetables you are eating?

Do you wear a red yarn bracelet to keep evil spirits away?

Have you had your house AND your car feng shui'ed?

Instead of taking vacations do you save money by just getting re-birthed?

Do you have solstice and equinox celebrations circled in red on your calendar?

Do you get 'TWO for ONE' colonic cleansing offers in the mail?

Do you look forward to ending each day with a wonderful wheat grass enema?

Our Church

The Organ Tuner

The church organ had been out of tune for over a year. Its off-key renderings had made the minister wince on more than one occasion. He finally broke down and called a man in to adjust the old organ.

An older white-haired man appeared at the church early the following day carrying his repair/tuning kit. The old man took one look at the aged organ and shook his head in pity. Then he took out his tools and worked at the organ steadily for the rest of the day.

After eight hours of solid work by the tuner the minister was getting really worried that the repair bill might be too steep. He was mightily relieved then as the old repairman finally finished, as it was getting dark. He was even more surprised as he looked at the cost of the repair bill - FIVE DOLLARS.

The minister had hoped for a church discount but this was too good to be true. He asked the old repairman,

"How can you make a decent living charging this much for a whole day's work?"

The old repairman just cupped one hand to his ear and replied,

"What?"

Termites

Our minister had the old church fumigated. The termites didn't die but instead moved to some dead trees in the back yard. That area became known as our church's arbor-eat'm.

Looking for a Church Property

A country-bred minister had recently arrived in New York City. He wanted to start a new church in the city and he had raised the money to do so before leaving his last congregation.

The minister sat down with a real estate agent and explained his dream and how he hoped the agent would be able to help him find the right property. The realtor listened for a few minutes and then told the minister to look through his book of listings. They would then make plans to visit his choices the next day.

The minister thanked the realtor and began to pour over thousands of pages of listings in the city. Two hours later the realtor checked on the minister who exclaimed,

"I think I've found it! This one sounds perfect."

The realtor peered at the chosen listing and read aloud,

'Large, open, airy floor plan - 15000 square foot building. Outstanding, Quaint, Old World charm in a convenient location . Includes adjacent cozy cottage. Security system in place. Move-in condition. Price reduced - Motivated seller.'

There was no picture of the property on the listing. The realtor found the property address and they agreed to meet at the property the next morning.

The following day the minister arrived at the address only to find a run down warehouse leaning on its side on a neglected lot. The realtor arrived a few minutes later and did his best to explain that listings in the big city are not <u>always</u> what that they seem and that:

It was open & airy - a wall was missing and the others were full of holes.
Outstanding - it was standing, though at an angle and like a sore thumb.
Quaint Old World charm - it was old, filthy and decrepit.
Convenient - it was located under a busy freeway.
The adjacent cozy cottage - was indeed cozy, it was a tiny shed.
Security System - the next-door neighbor had a dog.
Move in condition - meant the front door was missing.
Motivated seller - the property had been for sale for over ten years.

Church Bulletin items

Ladies, don't forget the church rummage sale. It's a chance to get rid of those things not worth keeping around the house. Bring your husbands.

Fund raiser. The ladies of the church have cast off clothing of every kind. They may be seen in the church hall on Saturday.

Don't let worry kill you. Let your church help.

The peace mediation training scheduled for today has been canceled due to a conflict.

Like-new mattress for sale. Slight urine smell.

Please ladies! Lend the pastor your electric girdles for the church's pancake breakfast next week.

The low-self-esteem group will meet this Friday in the church basement. Please use the back door.

Weight watchers group will meet at 7. Please use the large double doors at the side entrance.

Our Sunday school teens will be performing "Hamlet" next month. The congregation is invited to attend this tragedy.

Prayer and fasting retreat this weekend. Cost for attending includes all meals.

Morning sermon "Jesus walking on the water."
Evening sermon "Looking for Jesus."

Our friend Phyllis is in the hospital for an operation and is having difficulty sleeping. She requests copies of Reverend Tim's sermons.

Tryouts for the church choir next week. They need all the help they can get.

The evening sermon will be "What is Hell."
Please come early and listen to the choir.

A bean supper will be held Sunday night in the church hall.
Please stay to listen to the music afterwards.

Fred donated the new loudspeaker to the congregation –
In memory of his wife.

Good News - Bad News

An upbeat minister who ran the church's soup kitchen said a prayer before the evening meal. Afterwards he announced that there was some good news and some bad news about the evening meal.
First the bad news.

"Our weekly food shipment has been delayed and all we have to eat this evening is some leftover meatloaf that has started to go bad.
But, the good news is ... there is plenty of it to go around."

*****

On the way to church services with a busload of disabled members, the minister stood up to announce some good news and bad news.
First the bad.

"At our last stop a man got on board our bus and pulled out a gun. Our bus has been hijacked.
The <u>good</u> news is ... we seem to be headed toward the beach."

Church Rehab

The church was having a major renovation done. It was being repainted, two new bathrooms added, new flooring put in and the electrical system was being updated. The workmen arrived to begin the construction work but after a few hours the lady minister asked to speak to the foreman of the crew.

"Sir," she began, "this is a house of God and the profanity some of your men are using cannot be tolerated. There is to be no more swearing."

"But Reverend, these men are construction workers and you have to cut them some slack. I'll caution them but there's no getting round the fact that they will still call 'a spade a spade'."

"Sir, it is not the 'spade is a spade' business I am talking about. It's the 'f***ing shovel is a f***ing shovel' that I am talking about."

Church Secretary

The minister had hired a new church secretary. I asked him how she was working out?

"Fine, except she keeps saying I'm not broad-minded and expansive enough in my thinking."

"Why's that?"

"Because I believe words can only be spelled <u>one</u> way.

But, at least she's honest."

"Honest in what way?"

"Yesterday she called in <u>lazy</u>.

But, I may still need to let her go."

"Why's that?"

"She's in the habit of working eight hours and sleeping eight hours."

"What's wrong with that? I do it myself."

"The SAME eight hours?"

Broken Bus

The church group was coming back from a picnic in the Scottish countryside. All of a sudden there was a loud 'popping' sound from under the hood. The bus shuttered and then ground to a halt. Smoke was pouring from the engine. The minister took one look and knew they were in trouble.
Spying a small barn in the distant field, the minister headed in that direction by himself to find help. Next to the barn tending her chickens, he found an old lady. The minister waved his hand to get her attention and asked,

"Hello, is there a mechanic around here?"

To which she looked up and replied,

"No. But we do have a McSweeney and a McDuff down the road."

Job Interview

A young minister was being interviewed by the head of the church board for an opening as senior minister at a large country church. The interview seemed to be going well and the minister was asked what kind of compensation he might expect if hired? The young man thought for a second and answered that,

"Oh, about one hundred thousand dollars a year and benefits would be nice."

The head of the church board responded with,

"How would you feel about six weeks paid vacation a year, full medical coverage and a Mercedes convertible to drive around in?"

"Wow. Are you kidding?"

"Of course," replied the head of the board, "but you started it."

Church Definitions

Amen - the part of the prayer everybody knows.

Church Bulletin - church air conditioning.

Inner Peace - A short attention span.

Young Reverend Bob

Reverend Bob's parents were in the iron and steel industry. His mother ironed and his father stole.

*****

"Reverend Bob used to have a problem with biting his nails. But the congregation helped him to stop doing it."
"How did they do that?"
"They made him wear his shoes."

*****

Reverend Bob had an elderly church member named Mr. Skiddish who desperately needed a haircut. Reverend Bob decided to cut the man's hair himself. After he was done Mr' Skiddish asked for a drink of water.
Reverend Bob asked,
"Is your throat dry?'
"No. I just wanted to check for leaks."

*****

Reverend Bob decided to visit a church in Canada. He needed a new vehicle to get there and bought an electric car to save money on gas. The cost of the electricity for the trip was only $5. But the extension cords cost him $5,000.

*****

Reverend Bob went camping with the youth church group. He forgot to bring his pillow and went looking for something to rest his head on.
He reappeared at the campsite with a two foot length of drainage pipe under his arm
Elder Shane asked him,

"Isn't that pipe going to be a bit hard and uncomfortable for your neck?"

"Oh, I wasn't planning on using it just like this. I 'm going to stuff it with grass first."

At Bob's Bible College all students were ordered to change their underwear frequently. After a month there was still an unpleasant odor coming from Bob's room. The Dean of Students called Bob into his office and asked,

"Bob, are you changing your underwear every week as I directed?"

"Yes Dean. As a matter of fact I just changed the other day with my roommate Phil."

*****

"Reverend Bob is not as clumsy as people think."
"He's not?"
"No. He even invented a new dance.'
"Really. What's it called?"
"The Elevator."
"Why the Elevator?"
"Because it has no steps."

*****

The Dean asked Bob how he could possibly make so many mistakes?
The young man pondered the question and replied that,
"I get up very early."

*****

Reverend Bob and another minister, Rev. Pete went into town to watch the movie 'Seabisquit'.
Halfway through the movie Rev. Pete turned to Bob and told him he was willing to bet $10 that Seabisquit would win the next race in the movie. Reverend Bob accepted the bet. Seabisquit won and after the movie, Bob handed Rev. Pete $10.. Rev. Pete refused the money. He said he felt guilty about taking it because he had seen the same movie yesterday. Reverend Bob replied,
"I did too. But I didn't think he could win it two times in a row."

*****

Before he became a minister, Reverend Bob had a job in a Starbucks coffee shop.
But, they fired him because he kept coming to work in a 'T'-Shirt.

*****

What did Reverend Bob get on his S.A.T. Test?
Dandruff

"Reverend Bob, I think I met your brother after church services yesterday. He looks just like you but he's a lot shorter."

"Thats cuz he's my 'half brother."

*****

Reverend Bob tried to get a job in town as an elevator operator. He was fired because he had so much trouble trying to learn the route.

*****

Reverend Bob's dog was causing a lot of problems at the church picnic. The huge dog would chase everyone on a bicycle and knock them over. Reverend Bob solved the problem himself.
He took away the dog's bicycle.

*****

Reverend Bob was seen building a box two inches wide by two inches high and fifty feet long. A church member asked about the strange dimensions of the box? Rev. Bob explained that Brother Felix had been transferred to a new job in Florida and had asked Rev. Bob to ... please send him his garden hose.

*****

Reverend Bob tried to call 911 during an emergency. He dialed the nine okay but gave up when he couldn't find an <u>eleven</u> on the phone face.

*****

Reverend Bob wanted to do something to prove to everyone that he was a lot smarter than they thought he was. So, he decided to memorize the capital of every state in the United States. He studied diligently for almost a month and then after church one day, he told the congregation what he had accomplished. A church elder tested Rev. Bob by asking him to name the capital of Wisconsin?
Reverend Bob proudly enunciated "W".

*****

Reverend Bob had tried to make some money for the church by raising chickens. It didn't work out. He thinks he just planted them too deep.

Reverend Bob had a good friend who wanted to help make his life simpler and bought him a huge supply of paper plates. But Bob stopped using them after only a week because ... they were clogging up the dishwasher.

*****

Reverend Bob cooked a pot roast for six days in the oven because the instructions said to allow one hour for every pound.
And ... Bob weighed one hundred and forty pounds.

*****

At college Bob heard on a TV commercial that 'brushing alone will not prevent cavities.'
So, he only brushed his teeth when his roommate was around.

*****

Reverend Bob lost his part-time quality control job at the M & M's factory because he kept discarding all the 'W's.

*****

Reverend Bob sold his water skis because he couldn't find any lakes with a hill in them.

*****

Reverend Bob was staying at a fancy hotel in a large city. The desk clerk received a frantic call later that night from Bob saying that he couldn't get out of his room. The clerk asked Bob if he had tried to open the door.
Reverend Bob said,
"Yes. But the door only goes to the toilet."
"No," said the clerk, "I mean the door in the front of the room where you came in."
"Oh no," said Bob, " not the one that has the sign on it that says 'DO NOT DISTURB.'"

*****

Reverend Bob was in a terrible accident last week. He was in town and was hit by a truck that knocked him twenty feet in the air. The police arrived and instead of arresting the driver, they gave Bob a ticket for...
'leaving the scene of an accident'.

Reverend Bob went into town to get some pills for an elderly church member's sick poodle. The village veterinarian sent Bob back with some pink pills and within a week the poodle was almost well.
The elderly owner was pleased and when the pills ran out, he asked Bob to go back to the vet and get some more.

"By the way Reverend Bob, do you know what kind of pills they were? They sure worked well."

"I don't exactly know" replied Bob, "but I do know they taste a bit like licorice."

*****

Reverend Bob took his car into a local garage and asked the mechanic to fix a list of problems – and… would the man do it for free as a courtesy?

The mechanic looked at the repair list and reluctantly agreed to do them for free.

Reverend Bob picked up his car the next day and looked at his repair list and the mechanic's notes:

1. My left front tire almost needs replacement.
2. There is something loose under the hood.
3. There is evidence of a leak of some kind under the car.
4. The radio volume control is unbelievably loud.

Mechanic repair notes.

1. Almost repaired left front tire.
2. Something tightened under hood.
3. Evidence of leak removed.
4. Radio volume set more believably loud.

Signs that your Preacher may be a Redneck

1. He whistles to get everyone's attention.

2. He's been married more than once - and still has the same in-laws.

3. His kids light up and smoke during the service.

4. He likes to show off his tattoos between services.

5. The church bus's gas tank has a hose sticking out of it instead of a cap.

6. David slew Goliath. He did not "kick the crap out of him".

7. The church restroom sits out in the yard and alternates in pretty blue or orange colors.

8. He has two brothers who died right after yelling, "Hey guys watch this!"

9. He has 'personalized' license plates (they were made by his father).

10. He saves his clean bib-overalls just for Sunday services.

11. His idea of a seven-course dinner is a possum and a six-pack of beer.

12. The church has a front porch ... and under it live more than 5 dogs.

13. He cleans his fingernails with a stick.

14. He's in a custody fight over a hunting dog.

15. You notice his monster truck outside of Hooters every weekend.

16. The church's next fund-raiser involves raising worms.

17. He asks for prayer help to finance a tattoo.

18. His e-mail provider is OVERYONDER.COM.

19. Instead of Reverend, he prefers being called Billy-Bob.

20. Church services always end in time to get home to watch the football game.

21. The church salad bowls all have 'Cool Whip' on their sides.

22. To get into the church choir, there is a compulsory swimsuit competition.

23. You have an engine block for a church altar.

24. The last time he mowed his lawn, he found his missing wheelbarrow.

25. He shows up for the Sunday service in cut-offs and a tank top.

26. Instead of a cross above your altar, he has a velvet Elvis.

27. At home, he has to move the weed whacker to take a bath.

28. He performs wedding ceremonies in camouflage gear.

29. He waters his yard by unzipping first.

30. He ends each service with "y'all come back now Y'hear."

31. There is a spittoon on your altar.

32. The communion wine is mad dog 20/20.

33. The minister says that Adam and Eve were 'nekked'.

34. The handle on the church door is an old deer head.

35. Your church music includes Johnny Cash's 'Ring of Fire' and a chorus of 'dueling banjos'.

36. The corners of the church are held up by cinder blocks.

37. The church pews have vinyl seats.

38. The kids in Sunday school watch pay-for-view wrestling to dramatize bible stories.

39. The minister hiccups and his tobacco chaw slips out.

40. The church picnic features a bobbing for French fries in hot oil contest.

41. There is the logo of a major farm equipment company on the back of your minister's robe.

You Know Your Minister is Getting Too Heavy

1. When her electric bill goes up from over-use of the refrigerator light.

2. When she falls down, she winds up rocking herself to sleep trying to get up.

3. She has to have her garment bag let out.

4. Members of the congregation have to make two trips to hug all of her good-bye.

5. She moonlights as a 'lectern model'.

6. She donates her old clothes to HOUSE the homeless.

7. At church outings at the beach she wears a five-piece bikini.

8. Her favorite foods are 'seconds' and 'thirds'.

9. She has put on so much weight that the surround-sound from the entertainment center can no longer 'surround' her.

Quickie Puns

The cleaning lady at the church was just hospitalized with a rare case of double ammonia.

Adam and Eve's first argument was over who wore the plants in the family.

Did you see the movie about the cannibal that ate his Christian mother-in-law?
Its called 'Gladiator'.

There was an earthquake beneath the church. The minister announced it was not his fault.

The church elder complained that his wife was 'bi-sexual'.
She only liked to make love twice a year.

God went looking for his special apple in the Garden of Eden.
But it was a fruitless search.

An irritable lady minister from Georgia was put on a weight loss program known as the South Bitch Diet.

Marriage is an institution that separates the 'men from the joys'.

The dormitory at the Bible College exploded and there were a lot of roomers flying.

The minister drove the old church van for many years and said he would continue to do so until the day of wreckoning.

A lady minister was rear-ended in her car while she was putting on her mascara.
She came away suffering from whipped lashes.

The animals on Noah's ark didn't want to leave the ark when the flood abated because they liked their pier group.

A minister with bad teeth started his own Christian motorcycle club. He became known as the leader of the plaque.

A Lutheran minister by the name of Reverend Seymore Hinni is allegedly credited with the development of the miniskirt.

The minister refused to look at his wife's broken leg after she got back from the hospital because he thought they had said it was X-Ray-ted.

In the olden days sinners were dropped bodily into the fiery lava atop Mount Vesuvius.
When several Christians complained that this penalty was too harsh, the Roman emperor pronounced that he wanted to be make sure 'no misdeeds went unpumiced'.

After reading the Da Vinci Code a minister decided to write a sequel about the search for a missing tract of land on which Jesus lived. But in the end it didn't do well because there was no plot.

A lady minister married a Chinese Buddhist man because she liked the way he used his noodle.

Old Sunday school principals never die - they just lose their faculties.

A young minister fell into the church outhouse and drowned.
His cause of death was listed as 'sewercide'.

The new minister won first prize at the county fair milking contest. The humble man took his prize and told the crowd that he 'owed his success to udders.'

The congregation was told that their overweight minister had gone away to Las Vegas and had a big weekend. The church elder replied that he knew the minister had a big end but that he hadn't known that it was weak as well.

The minister claimed that his new bloodhound could retrieve a stick thrown all the way across the river. The congregation thought that the story was a bit far fetched.

The minister said his new hairpiece was like living with a lie.
It was a false hood.

Why are Jehovah's Witnesses like a flock of raucous crows?
Because they like to hear their cause heard.

A favorite lady minister of ours loves to read romantic novels about adventurous women.
We often refer to her as the heroine addict.

Two lady ministers had the bizarre practice of exchanging skunks on St.Valentines Day.
One of the ladies explained that they did it because they were so scent-imental.

The minister sent his girlfriend one of his paintings on Valentines Day because he wanted her to know that he cared about her ... 'with all his art'.

The old gambler was upset when the minister told him he could not marry the rich widow until they had known each other longer. The old man told the minister that an exception had to be made for him because it was a matter of ... wife and debt.

A minister noticed a widowed friend of his and his dog entering the church graveyard.
He walked up to the man, who was dressed in black, and greeted him, "Morning."
"No, just walking the dog."

A lady minister in Hollywood kept two brand new brooms over her fireplace mantle. A friend asked about them. She explained that they made her feel better because she knew that at least *they* hadn't swept together.

Our church served natural grain bread with small holes in at every church breakfast.
The new minister asked about the holes.
We told him that hole wheat bread was our favorite.

The cannibal complained to the village witchdoctor that he got indigestion whenever he tried to eat a Christian missionary. The old witchdoctor explained that it was often difficult to keep a good man down.

A church in the Ozarks was having a problem with church members who were making and selling illegal moonshine. The minister was asked to condemn the practice from the pulpit and let everyone know that the church could not condone such whiskey business.

A lady minister was asked what she had liked best about her visit to Italy. "Oh, I just loved visiting all those ancient Roman fornifications."

The minister slept with a flashlight under his pillow. His wife complained that he was a light sleeper.

Someone started a rumor that their rich new minister slept in a luxurious bed that was the size of an entire house. The congregation thought that was a lot of bunk.

The minister had been married six times and was now considered 'spouse-broken."

The shy minister had a high moralistic opinion of himself and liked to refer to himself as the 'mighty rock' of his church family.
His girlfriend just wished he were a little boulder.

The minister who liked to garden around the church met a very charming woman at a retreat.
But she refused to date him because he was known to be a little rough around the hedges.

The old minister had met and married a much younger woman of somewhat loose virtues.
They became known as a fastidious couple. She was fast and he was tedious.

Reverend Sharpy was seriously injured while crossing some railroad tracks. He was taken to a hospital where the entire left side of his body was amputated. He's all <u>right</u> now.

A little boy refused to admit that he had eaten a tub of glue at Sunday school. Even though there were many witnesses, his lips were sealed.

What do you call a prophet who can tell the future by just looking up your nose?
Nostrildamus.

The minister liked to talk about the forceful image of God in theOld Testament.
A God who was stern and all-noing.

Did you here about the evangelist who invented lighter fluid. He became flamous.

Then there was a minister who liked to construct bathroom hardware. He isn't famous but is known for forging a head.

After Adam and Eve were forced out of the Garden of Eden they had to start covering their nakedness. Their children's' clothes were the first leaflets.

Herod the Great constructed the Temple of Jerusalem. He also built the first marble church.
But he had troubles with it because it just kept ... rolling away.

When that first marble church was completed, everybody took it for granite.

The new minister acted awfully big for his britches but it left him exposed in the end.

The minister's dog gave birth to twelve puppies at the shopping mall. Instead of helping him with the brood, the security guard gave him a ticket for... littering.

The lonely minister bought a large dog and named it Ben. On her first trip to the veterinarian's office she found out the dog was a female. She renamed it Ben Her.

The church choir room was broken into. At first they thought all the musical instruments had been saved from the thieves. But the next day they realized the thieves had gotten away with the lute.

Did you know that Moses was the first prophet to advocate the use of toilet paper?
Until then his followers really had it rough.

Do you know why Jesus left his occupation as a carpenter?
Because he liked to bite his nails.

The apostle Simon ran a successful shoe store. He was known to have a lot of sole.

A tribe of cannibals in New Guinea played a horrible game that involved killing and eating the missionaries who arrived to run the jungle church. They called it 'swallow the leader.'

The church's youth ministers decided to participate in a 100 mile bicycle marathon for charity.
They came in first place and as a reward were given a weak end off.

Pessimistic ministers have the odd habit of wearing sunglasses during Sunday services.
This is because they prefer to take a dim view of things.

The minister and his wife decided to buy a waterbed.
It didn't help their sleeping, and they soon drifted apart.

Monty the new minister liked to sleep under the church bus at night because he liked to get up oily in the morning.

Bumper Sticker: Man who jog behind church bus - get exhausted.

The minister invested church money to buy an indoor jogging machine for his church members. He wanted them to get a good run for their money.

If Noah had built his ark out of stone instead of wood, it might have been a hard ship.

A minister we know tries to appeal to his younger members by standing on a skateboard during his sermons. It turned out to be a wheely bad idea.

Our church organist liked to talk about her music <u>and</u> do spiritual counseling after services.
She was said to give sound advice.

Ministers visiting India were told to be very careful not to get sick at the airport because they didn't want any terminal illnesses.

The navy chaplain gave a Sunday sermon on the battleship. Participants received a fine deck-oration.

The minister's wife used to sell neckties for a living. She was said to know how to collar a man.

When two egotistical ministers meet it is said to be an 'I' for an "I".

The Reverend Jim Baker of PTL finally got out of prison. His new wife asked him why he insisted on sleeping under the bed at night. He explained that he just wanted to lay low for a while.

The minister's wife ordered a python as a pet from the back of a magazine. When the package arrived it contained only a plastic snake.
It seems the 'boa cons tricked her.'

A bi-polar minister believes in 'easy glum, easy glow.'

Spiritually minded people are known to be quite amen-able.

The church choir director kept throwing tempo tantrums.

A minister was de-frocked because of his preoccupation with women's bosoms.
He was diagnosed as being a 'cleftomaniac'.

Saint Joan of Arc was burned to a steak.

An arsonist asked for the congregation's forgiveness saying 'I who have singed'.

The minister was a bit of a hypochondriac - he wouldn't leave 'well enough' alone.

The cross-eyed minister wasn't allowed to teach any school classes because she had a.... hard time controlling her pupils.

The new minister claimed that all the mistakes in his sermons were merely clerical errors.

An Amish girl heard that her boyfriend's car needed a new muffler. So she knitted one for him.

Adam and Eve ran a little grocery store after their expulsion from the Garden of Eden.
On its door was a sign stating, 'WE ARE NEVER CLOTHED.'

One of the ministers avoided every funeral service because he was not a mourning person.

The minister spilled coffee on his wife and she showed him dis-stain.

The minister's younger daughter was living with a common-law husband. He didn't approve but tried to be cordial. He slipped a bit that year at Thanksgiving dinner when he called the man his Sin-in-Law.

A minister had been placed in a nursing home and was refusing to take his afternoon nap.
The police were called in and they told the man to take his nap or he would be charged with resisting a-rest.

The woman explained to the minister that she had not been to church lately because she was having problems with a terrible skin condition. He chastised her anyway and told her that it was a pore excuse.

The minister's girlfriend refused to marry him because of 'religious differences'.
She worshipped money and he didn't have any.

Why is a visiting preacher like a house ablaze?
The sooner they are put out, the better.

The minister ate blue eggs every morning for breakfast, lunch and supper.
He was on a dye-it.

PETS

Roosters

The country minister liked to raise chickens in back of his house. A new rooster he had just purchased was exploring the yard when the old rooster marched over to him and said,

"You don't look like you've got what it takes to rule this yard. I'll bet you a cup of corn that I can outrun you."

The new rooster raised up his feathers and accepted the bet. The old rooster took off in at a full tilt and the new rooster followed in hot pursuit.

As they turned the corner of the house the minister was outside watching. The minister lifted a pistol from his lap and taking careful aim - shot the new rooster dead.

"Darn it," cursed the minister, " that's the third queer rooster I've bought this month!"

Family Cat

The minister's wife took the family's male cat into the vet to have it neutered.

The vet performed the procedure and told the wife that the operation was successful 95% of the time.

The minister's wife asked how she would know for sure because they didn't want any more kittens.

The vet said to just observe the cat. And if it started acting too 'male', bring it back in.

"Do you mean like lying around on the couch all day in front of the television?"

"No. That would still be appropriate. But if he starts hogging the remote, bring him in."

The Parrot #1

A burglar broke into the minister's house while his family was at Sunday service. Finding the house empty, he was quietly unloading the kitchen silverware into his bag when a deep voice called out,

"Jesus is watching you!"

The burglar froze in his tracks but when silence returned, decided he would continue helping himself to the cutlery.

"Jesus is watching you!' came the voice again.

Frightened out of his wits, the man looked carefully around him. He seemed to be alone in the kitchen except for a large parrot in a cage. Looking closely at the parrot, he asked the bird if it had spoken. The bird answered,

"YES."

Breathing a sigh of relief, the burglar asked the bird if it had a name.

"Yes," said the bird, "its Stinker."

"Stinker' laughed the burglar, "that's a stupid name. What jerk gave you a name like that?"

"The same jerk who named that Doberman over there 'Jesus'."

Church Dog

We are having a problem with our church dog.
What kind of problem?
He's a husky and he likes to hang around with wolves.
Do they attack him?
No.
Then what's the problem?
He's up to three packs a day.

The Parrot#2

Our minister received a package from his missionary son in Africa. Inside was a beautifully colored parrot with a note wishing the father a happy birthday. Our minister was thrilled with the gift until he tried to get the parrot to speak.

From the parrot's mouth came a string of profanity and cussing that turned the air blue! Doing his best to quiet the outrageous bird, he wondered what to do. First he tried prayer, but the bird's language only seemed to get worst. Then he tried patience and gently spoke only loving words to the bird for over a month.

At the end of the month he cautiously offered the parrot a cracker. Again he was met with loud expletives. Just then, he heard a female member of the church board being greeted by his wife at the door. He panicked and threw the still-cussing bird into the refrigerator.

After the lady board member left, he retrieved the parrot. The shivering bird stepped out onto his proffered arm and spoke,

"I wish to extend my apology for my crude language..."

Our minister was pleased and a bit taken aback by the quick change. Then the bird continued,

"And may I ask what rude thing did that stupid chicken in the fridge say?"

PARROT #3

The son of a poor but religious widow struck it rich and sent his mother a rare parrot that cost over $90,000. because it could recite bible passages and all Ten Commandments. He called to ask her how she liked the rare bird. Her answer,

"It was delicious. Thank you son."

FLEAS

The minister's dog was given garlic pills to get rid of its fleas. It worked, but now its bark is much worse than its bite.

Christian Dating Lines

"Hi, is this pew taken?

"I'd like to pray with you."

"Do you believe God has directed us to be together?"

"I know a church where we can go to talk."

"You know Jesus? Me too!"

"God told me to come talk to you."

"Is it a sin that you stole my heart?"

"Nice bible."

"Have you ever tried praying at the drive in movies?"

"My prayers are answered!"

"I think you are sitting on my Bible."

"Have you read any good passages lately?"

"Do you worship here often?"

TEXAS

Texan in Paris

A Baptist minister from Texas was visiting Paris with his wife for the first time. His brother-in-law Pierre had been born in France and was serving as a tour guide for the couple. As they went by the Eiffel Tower Pierre pointed it out and explained how it had been constructed in less than two years.

"Shoot," said the Texas minister, "a little old tower like that we could put up in under two weeks in Texas."

Next they drove by Notre Dame Cathedral and Pierre described how it had taken hundreds of years to finally finish the construction, but that it was now the largest cathedral in Europe.

"Shucks said the Texan. We could build something like that in under a year in Texas."

Pierre was now visibly getting a little upset with his boorish visitor. But saying nothing he continued their tour out into the countryside. Coming to the top of a small hill the sprawling majesty of the palatial homes of King Louis and Napoleon at Versailles came into view.

"Wowww! " said the Texas minister, "What's that over there?'

Pierre replied with a smile,

"Damned if I know. Wasn't there yesterday."

Too Raw

A Baptist minister from Texas was visiting New York City for the first time. He joined some friends at a fancy restaurant near Central Park for dinner. They each ordered the largest steak on the menu.

The steaks arrived but the minister looks at his and sends it back saying it is too raw. The waiter takes the steak back to the kitchen. The waiter returns with the steak and tells the minister that the cook assures him the steak is properly cooked.

The minister looks disgustedly at the steak and tells the waiter to take it back again and relay the following message to the cook.

'I'm from Texas and I've often seen cows hurt much worse than this - and they recovered!'

Texas Evangelist

A prominent Texas evangelist and his wife were on a vacation tour of the U.S. Late one afternoon he stopped his big S.U.V. outside a small Amish farm in Pennsylvania. A bearded Amish farmer saw the huge S.U.V. outside and went out to invite the two strangers in for something to eat.

After a delicious dinner the Texan complimented the Amish farmer on the quality of the food served by his wife. He also mentioned that he too, was a farmer and was curious about how large the Amish farmer's 'spread' might be.

The Amish farmer scratched his head and replied that his farm was about one hundred acres in all. Then to be polite, he asked the tall Texan about the size of his farm.

"Well," said the Texan, puffing up mightily and hitching up his belt, "I wake up in the morning and after a good breakfast, I jump on my favorite horse and ride all day - and at the end of the day I finally reach the edge of my farm."

To this the Amish farmer nodded knowingly and said,

"Yes, I know. I used to have a horse like that too..."

OLDEN TIMES

Bread and Turnips

In Victorian England, an elderly hermit was starving on his small rocky farm. Packing up his meager belongings, he began the long trek into the nearest city. Arriving at the city's great cathedral, he was told that there was free food being given away.

The hermit approached the massive doors of the cathedral and asked the florid-faced minister in the entry.

"Can I have some bread and turnips?"

No, explained the minister. The food was distributed at the cathedral only on Sundays. Since this was Tuesday, the man must wait.

The next day the hermit returned to the cathedral and asked,

"Can I have some bread and turnips?"

The minister was a bit perturbed, but did his best to explain that the man must wait four more days until Sunday.

The next day the hermit was again at the cathedral in front of the minister.

"Can I have some bread and turnips?"

The minister was now angry.
"No! You cannot have any bread or turnips - and if you ask me that one more time, I'll have you nailed up onto the doors as a lesson to all foolish peasants!"

The little hermit left. But, the next day he was again in front of the cathedral. The minister looked up and slammed his fist down onto his desk and seethingly asked what the hermit wanted.

"Do you have any nails?"

This caught the minister by surprise and he had to think for a second before answering,

"NO, we don't have any nails. Anything else?"

"Then, can I have some bread and turnips?"

Time Machine

A minister, who was also a scientist, constructed a time machine in the church basement. He used it to go back in time to return to the time of Jesus.

He arrived a bit late but was in time to see Jesus resurrecting from the tomb. The minister's heart was filled and his faith renewed. But before leaving the scene he felt a deep desire to share this moment with his congregation.

He had taken along a camera and he gingerly approached the shining newly risen Christ and asked Jesus if he would mind having a few pictures taken?

Jesus consented graciously and posed for several shots while the minister clicked away. The minister thanked Jesus when he was done and got back into his time machine. Upon his return the minister tried to develop the pictures but they were all blank.

The minister re-checked his camera and found that the flash batteries were all drained. Though disappointed, he realized he had at least proven the old adage,

"THE SPIRIT IS WILLING BUT, THE FLASH IS WEAK."

The Old West

A wandering preacher in the days of the old west had a talking dog of which he was very proud. One day the dog disappeared. The preacher grieved for his missing dog and offered up prayers for its safe return.

After three weeks he heard that his talking dog had been seen limping into a nearby town using only three legs. The dog had dragged its tired body and useless fourth leg into the town's only saloon and had explained loudly to the patrons that,

"I'M LOOKING FOR THE MAN THAT SHOT MY PAW!"

Path Finding

A preacher in the Oregon territories in the 1800's came upon an American Indian brave lying on the ground with his ear pressed into the dirt.

A whisper came from the Indian's lips, as the minister got closer.

"Six men, on horses with carriage and two squaws."

'Wow," said the preacher, "you can tell all that just from listening to the ground?"

"Unh..Unh.." replied the Indian, "They just run over me."

Early Christians

The minister was trying to explain to the Sunday school class how difficult were the times in which the Early Christians lived. He explained how the very first Christians had no machines to make their lives easier.

To wash things they had to take them down to the river wrapped in sheets and slam them against the rocks until they were clean.

To which, little Reggie replied,

"Wow! That must have been murder on the dishes."

THANKSGIVING

The Indian shaman knew his people were in trouble at that first
Thanksgiving when the pilgrims started to sing,

"This land was your land, this land is my land."

Last Thanksgiving, I decided to go out and shoot my own turkey.
It was fun.
But, now they won't let me back into the grocery store.

If you want something a little different for Thanksgiving dinner this year,
try swan. They roast well and hold a lot more stuffing.

This year we decided to celebrate Thanksgiving in a more traditional way
 (like our forefathers).
We invited everyone in the neighborhood to our house for an enormous
home-cooked feast...
Then afterwards, wed took their land.

CHRISTMAS STORIES

Holy Moley

There was a large family of moles who lived on the church grounds. The father mole, his wife and their twenty children including the youngest, little Bobby, would come out of their mole-hole every Sunday when church was in session. The entire mole family would stand together next to their hole with their little paws folded and their heads reverently bowed.

The minister of the church noticed this odd behavior and many in his congregation commented about their newest 'members'.

The minister and his congregation decided to do something special for the reverent little mole family that Christmas. They would secretly decorate the little fir tree that sat next to the mole hole in front of the church. So, on Christmas Eve, the minister and several volunteers arrived with colored lights, candy canes, sugarplums and other goodies and proceeded to decorate the little outside tree.

On Christmas morning the father mole got up early and squeezing up through the long mole tunnel to daylight observed the wondrous sight of the dazzling little tree. Rushing back down the mole hole, he woke his family with the news.

Each of the moles rushed to their tunnel and struggled to squeeze upward past each other to see this new wonder. The father and mother mole got up first and looked in wonder at the twinkling lights.

The girl moles arrived next and admired the wrapped presents and tree garlands.

The little boy moles were next squeezing up the crowded mole-hole except for Bobby, who was the youngest and slowest. The boy moles were especially taken by the smell and sight of the candy canes and sugarplums.

But for little Bobby mole, the only thing he would remember from that Christmas day were ...

The Molasses.

The Three Wise Men

A man from Massachusetts was visiting friends in a small southern town in Georgia. It was almost Christmas and the town's people had erected a beautiful nativity scene in front of the town hall.

The depiction of Joseph and Mary and baby Jesus in the Manger brought back pleasant memories. It would have been a perfect memory of his youth except for the fireman's helmets worn by the three Magi.

He asked his friend about the helmets. Weren't they able to find more suitable headgear for the three wise men?

His friend just laughed and replied,

"Don't you Yankees ever read your bibles?'

He assured her that they did indeed read their bibles. But to the best of his memory, there was no mention of firemen at Jesus' birth.

His friend just happened to have her bible in her backpack and took it out. She thumbed to the relevant page and pointed out the appropriate passage for him.

He looked at the page in wonder and read,

"The three wise men came from 'afar'."

HMO's

Every time the minister told the Christmas story about Mary and Joseph having to deliver the baby Jesus in a manger, the congregation wondered whether maybe it was because they had the same kind of medical plans back then.

Heard in Minister's Counseling Sessions

"Reverend, My husband thinks he is a refrigerator."

"That is a little odd. But does he treat you with respect and honor your spiritual vows?"

"Yes, that part is fine. But it's at night when he sleeps with his mouth open. That little light keeps me awake."

"I had a lengthy operation for gallstones. The operation was successful but I think the surgeon may have left a sponge inside of me."

"Why do you think that? Are you having pains?"

"No. But boy do I get thirsty."

"I got my wife a lovely ladies wristwatch for her birthday.
 But she still won't speak to me."

"Didn't she like it?'

"Yes. But then the lady came and took it back."

A man walks into the minister's office for spiritual counseling He has a carrot up his nose, a green bean in his left ear and some celery in his right ear. He looks at the minister and asks,

"Reverend, I don't seem to have any energy lately. I don't have any interest in my wife and I don't even want to get up to go to work in the morning. What's wrong with me?"

"You're not eating properly."

An elderly gentleman confided to the minister that,

"Reverend, I have lived a good life but I wish to confess that during the big tornado last week a beautiful young girl came to my door and asked me to hide her from the storm. She was not a Christian but I let her in anyway and let her stay in my basement bedroom."

The minister responded, "Even though the girl was not of our faith, it was your Christian responsibility to help her and you committed no sin in taking her in."

"No," said the old man. "It was much worse than that Reverend. I allowed the young girl to repay me with sexual favors."

The minister recoiled a bit before saying,

"What you did then was sinful but, I can understand that under the circumstances ... being under the same roof together ... that these things happen. So, if you are truly sorry for what happened, I'm sure God will forgive you."

The old man sighed with relief and then continued,

"One more thing Reverend?"

"Yes?" said the minister.

"Should I tell her the storm is over?"

A neurotic young man came to our minister for counseling saying,

"Reverend, I have this terrible feeling that everyone is trying to take advantage of me."

Our minister told him to relax and not worry. These feelings were perfectly normal and that we all had them at times.
The young man breathed a sigh of relief and asked how much he should donate to the church for this very helpful session?
Our minister replied

"How much have you got?"

Poison

A man goes to see our minister to complain that he thinks his wife is trying to poison him. Our minister is shocked and asks the man how this could possibly be. The man is adamant and says,

"I just know that my food doesn't taste right and that she is trying to kill me."

Our minister tries to reassure him and says that he will talk to the wife and get to the bottom of this so that the man can stop worrying.

The following day our minister calls the man back into his office and tells him that after having spent several hours with the wife the previous night, he had some advice for him.

"Take the poison."

Knowing your mate

Fred and his wife June were in the minister's office for some marital counseling. Fred thought the relationship was fine but June complained that they never talked.

The minister explained to both of them how important it is to communicate and get to know those things that are important to each other.

Fred just laughed and said that they talked plenty and his wife was just making a mountain out of a molehill.

Noticing June's growing anger, the minister asked Fred if he could name and describe June's favorite flower.

"Sure, sure," said Fred. He thought for a moment and then leaned over to whisper in June's ear,

"It's Pillsbury, isn't it?"

And thus began Fred's life of celibacy.

Crazy?

A former member of the Hari Krishna's was sent by his wife to seek counseling from our minister. Our minister did his best to make the young man feel comfortable and then asked him why he thought his wife had sent him in for counseling?

The Hari Krishna scratched his bald scalp and replied that he wasn't sure - but he thought it might have something to do with his preference for sandals over closed-toe shoes.

"Why that's no Problem," exclaimed our minister.
"As a matter of fact, I prefer sandals myself.

"Really," replied the young man,

"Do you like yours boiled, smoked or pan-fried?"

The Heavenly 'Baker'

Genesis - in the beginning there were no cookies.

Adam & Eve - took a bite out of the first cookies.

Noah - liked two chocolate chip, two mallomars, two
    oreos, two sugar cookies .....

Moses - commanded the cookies to 'part'.

Atheists - there is no cookie baker.

Evolutionists - the cookies make themselves.

Buddhists - to die with no cookies.

Hinduism - no beef on my cookies please.

Confucianism - if the cookie gets wet, it is no longer dry.

Muslim - he, who breaks the most infidel cookies, wins.

Judaism - he who follows the recipe wins.

Mormons - boys can have as many cookies as they want.

Jehovah's witness - sell their cookies door to door.

Calvinists - you must earn your cookies.

Christian science - keep your cookies healthy.

Seventh Day Adventists - like their cookies best on Saturdays.

Baptists - prefer their cookies dipped in water.

Catholics - he who denies himself the most cookies, goes to Heaven.

Stoicism - I broke my cookie, but I can handle it.

Communism - share your cookies.

Polytheism - there are many bakers.

Capitalism - more cookies please.

Rastafarianism - I prefer to smoke my cookies.

Frisbeetarianism - when you die, your cookie gets stuck up on the roof.

Favorite Sermons

"The bible tells us that 'blessed are the merciful'.
This sermon is now over."

****

The secret of a good sermon is to have a good beginning and a good
ending.... and to have the two as close together as possible!

****

On a beautiful Sunday morning the wise old minister addressed the
congregation and announced that he had prepared three different sermons.
A $1000 sermon that lasts five minutes, a $500 sermon that lasts thirty
minutes and a $100 sermon that lasts a full hour.

"We will now take up a collection to decide which one gets delivered
today."

****

After the sermon, only one man applauded. And he was slapping his head
to keep himself awake.

****

After the service, the entire irreverent congregation was hissing at the
new minister. Except for one man's clapping. And he was applauding
the hissing.

Criss - Crossing

What do you get when you cross a Jehovah's Witness with a Unitarian Universalist?
Someone who knocks on your door for no particular reason...

What do you get when you cross a praying mantis with a termite?
An insect that says grace before eating the church.

What do you get when you cross a Southern Baptist minister and a barn owl?
A Fundamentalist who doesn't give a hoot.

Professor 'God'

Professor 'God' was recently fired from a major university because he:

Had only one major publication.

Some doubt he even wrote it himself.

When part of his 'experiment' wasn't turning out right, he drowned the sample.

He rarely came to class and just told his students to read the book.

It was said that he had his son teaching some of his classes.

He expelled his first two students for learning.

His office hours were very limited and held only on a mountaintop.

Potpourri

"Did you hear Ralph snoring in church this morning?"
"Sure did - he woke me up twice!"

"Minister, my wife doesn't understand me. Does yours?"
The minister. "I don't think she even knows you."

A less than tidy missionary with poor hygiene was coaxed
by the other missionaries to buy some 'odor-eaters' for his sandals.
It didn't work out. They 'ate' for a minute, then they threw up.

The minister who was caught spending too much time rehearsing
his sermons was admonished for, 'practicing what he preaches'.

The minister was upset when he found out that one of the donated books
for the church rummage sale was titled 'Pathways to Petting'.
That was, until someone showed him it was part of an..... Encyclopedia.

The church was having a funeral for the man who had invented the 'hokey
pokey' dance. The service went fine but something strange happened when
it came time for the burial... First they put his left foot in.....

Our latest statistics show that the Catholic Church must be doing
something right - their priests have the lowest divorce rate in the country!

The minister explained that the secret to his long successful marriage was
that he and his wife took two nights a week off to go out to a nice dinner
followed by dancing and cocktails... "My wife goes on Monday, I go on
Fridays."

The rich old church Elder was believed to be loosening his purse strings when he pledged $5oo,ooo. to the church building fund. At the end of the year, the minister still had not received the money and sent a note telling the man his pledge was a year old. The reply came back a week later - 'Happy Birthday!'

God heals - doctors collect the Fees.

Honesty pays - but not enough to suit most people.

Which is worst, death or taxes? At least death isn't an annual event.

Without sin, there would be a problem with unemployed clergy.

The Baptist minister's wife got her birth control pills mixed up with her Valium. They now have twenty children - but she just doesn't care.

The young minister was an incurable optimist. One day he was asked if there was anything positive about getting Alzheimer's disease. After some thought he replied...
"You are always meeting new people."

Our Church is open to all denominations - but it prefers 10's and 20's.

New church choir member: "I love to sing but don't know what to do with my hands?"
Choir director: "How about putting them over your mouth?"

"Dear God. Remember last year when you saved me from bankruptcy and I told you I would never forget you?'
"Well God. I'm broke again."

How to make God chuckle

1. Say you 'think the doctor cured you'.

2. Tell him 'your plans'.

3. Say to anything 'this is mine'.

4. Say to any situation 'I understand".

5. Complain that today it was 'hot out'.

More Puns

Reverend Abrupt was giving his choir director Ruth a ride home from church on his Vespa motor scooter. He had a bit of a reputation as a speed demon and Ruth kept her eyes closed as he wheeled around successive curves. Reverend Abrupt didn't see the bump in the road as he hit it – They bounced and he just continued on 'ruthlessly'.

A cannibal was expelled from bible school for buttering up his teacher.

The young woman's family failed to make a donation to the church after the minister performed an exorcism - so the poor woman was re-possessed.

Then, there was the missionary sent to convert the savages in darkest Africa. He showed up late for a special dinner with the cannibal tribe and was given the cold shoulder.

They are having a funeral today for a dead Angel.
It was said the Angel died of Harp failure.

The well-versed bible scholar was in the hospital recovering from a bad case of the flu. While there, he received a letter addressed to the 'ill literate'.

They've started a new organization for those that don't like to attend church. It's called the 'Seventh-day Absentists'.

The missionary was trying to help the sobbing cannibal.
"What's wrong?' inquires the missionary.
"I passed my brother in the jungle yesterday."

There was a church member who was a tailor who didn't like to charge for his services because he liked to work 'off the cuff'.

He remained a tailor his whole life because he 'seamed' to do so well.

At Christmastime he always asked only for a thimble because he didn't want to get 'stuck' without one.

The new minister had been kneeling in prayer all day with several of his congregation. Getting up finally, he went to a nearby cabinet and took out a Scrabble game so that they all could.... sit down for a spell.

A minister left his church in Greece and moved to America because he was tired of listening to lyres.

A man walks into a church with a piece of asphalt under his arm and gets in line for coffee at the end of the service.
The man receives his cup of coffee and asks the minister for a second cup.
The minister sees he hasn't even drunk from his first cup and asks why he wants a second cup?
The man says he wants one for the road.

Another man gets into the coffee line at the end of the service holding a jumper cable. When the man with the cable gets to the front of the line the minister says,

" Okay, okay, I'll serve you. Just don't start anything!"

The Baptist minister placed his teenage son in a weight training program because he wanted him to spend more time in an 'uplifting' environment.

A clergyman noted for his poor memory was warmly greeted on the street by a member of his congregation. Shaking the man's hand, he replied,

"I can't remember your name but your faith is familiar."

Church termites never die. They just go on living happily every 'rafter'.

The Baptist minister visiting Texas ordered ice cream with his pie for dessert because he wanted to 'Remember the A la mode.'

A Texas minister recently was granted a divorce from his wife after he found his 'dear and an interloper at play'.

The minister went on a diet because he was 'thick and tired of it'.

Our favorite minister had a special drawer for all his bills marked 'due unto others.'

Just before the great flood, Noah was heard remarking ungrammatically, "Now I herd everything."

The minister liked to publish as much gossip as possible in the church bulletin because he wanted to 'write others wrongs.'

Another minister decided to take three collections at every Sunday service instead of one because he didn't want to 'put all his begs in one basket'.

Lutheran pastors in Germany are called German shepherds.

The most successful banker in the bible was the Egyptian pharaoh's daughter because she went down to the Nile River and drew out a little prophet.

There was a near-sighted missionary who walked right through the church's screen door and 'strained' himself.

Our minister just returned from a vacation to Scotland. He brought back with him some very tasty cheese for the after-service social. When asked what type of cheese it was, he claimed it to be...
'Loch Ness muenster'.

The minister left the church's New Year's Eve masquerade party early because he was having a hard time telling the...
'Good guise from the bad'.

Above the door of a church in Alaska:
'Many are cold, but few are frozen."

Our church recently started a twelve-step program for compulsive talkers ...... it's called 'on and on anon'.

An elderly woman confessed to her minister that she was having a
recurring dream in which she was painting everything in sight with gold
paint. The minister told her not to worry. It was only her 'gilt complex'.

Our interdenominational get-together and prayer meeting attracted an
especially large attendance this year. Some say it was because of the new
promotional flyer that proclaimed...
Come and 'get to know the opposite sects'.

The new union for ministers is called,
The National Association for the Advancement of Collared People.

Atheism is a non-prophet organization.

The favorite Christmas carol at the Christian nudist camp was
 'Stark the Herald Angels sing'.

The name of the weight lifting team at the southern Baptist church was
the...'Brawn again Christians'.

The neighboring town's church had a new furnace installed.
Its members began referring to themselves as...
'Warm again Christians'.

Not to be outdone, the Baptist church downriver enticed a famous
hairdresser to join their congregation and they are now known as the .....
'Shorn again Christians'.

A southern Baptist minister had a habit of spending his Sunday afternoons at the automobile races. He said he doesn't gamble but just goes to experience the...'Rev-elation'.

A woman minister we know was fond of knitting while driving her car. One day she sped through a stoplight and a cop drove up next to her and yelled for her to "pull over!" She hollered back, "Nope, it's just a scarf."

The minister had a real interest in modern science. He was reading a book about anti-gravity and wound up reading all night and not getting any sleep. He said the reason was that he just 'couldn't put it down'.

Female ministers visiting Arab countries have long been encouraged to wear skirts that are unfashionably long. Because they cover a 'multitude of shins'.

A minister of German heritage was caught in an old fashioned Oklahoma blizzard. The car he was driving was an inexpensive foreign make and its windshield wipers were having a hard time keeping up with the driving wet snow. Finally the frail little wipers blew off completely in a powerful gust of wind.

The resourceful minister pondered for a moment. He couldn't continue on without something to clear his windshield. It was getting colder by the minute and he had a marriage ceremony to perform in the next town.

Hopping out of the car and into the storm, the minister strode out into a field next to the road and tipped over a large flat rock. Underneath it was a pile of hibernating rattlesnakes. Grabbing two of the larger snakes, he took them back to his car and installed one each - on the two empty blade holders.

He arrived in town just in time for the marriage ceremony. A curious guest noticed the snakes on the minister's car and asked him about them.

"Vat's the matter. You never heard of vind-chilled vipers?'

The largest Presbyterian Church in St. Louis, Mo. decided to hire a Scottish painting company to repaint the entire exterior of the church. The owner of the painting company, Mr. Pat McGroin, was officially a member of the congregation but, it had been many years since he had been seen at any services.

McGroin was a skilled painter but was known to be a bit tight when it came time to pay his bills or donate to the church. that aside, McGroin arrived bright and early to begin the job and started putting up ladders, scaffolding and lifts.

when it came time to buy the white paint, McGroin tried to order the exact amount. But when he got back to the site, he realized it wouldn't be enough. Instead of going back to the store for more paint, mcGroin waited until no one was looking and added a couple of gallons of paint thinner to each can to stretch the coverage.

McGroin spent the rest of the day painting and was almost finished when the sky darkened and a heavy rain began falling. He watched helplessly as the thunder rumbled and the fresh new paint began to drip.

The drips became puddles, the puddles merged into streams and soon the entire lawn and driveway of the church were covered in the telltale white blotches.

McGroin knew inside that this was a judgment from God to punish his act of skullduggery. Bemoaning his fate, McGroin threw himself to the ground with fists raised to heaven and prayed for forgiveness crying,

"Oh God, I am truly sorry. What can I do to make it up to you."

The thunder quelled and a powerful voice from above spoke,

"Repaint and Thin No more."

Golf

"Reverend. Is it a sin for me to play golf on Sundays?"

"The way you play, it is a sin ANY day."

Our minister asked if there were any six-year-old caddies for his golf bag.

"Six year old caddies? Wouldn't you prefer someone more mature?"

"No, I'm just looking for someone who can't count past ten."

One of the ladies in the foursome admired the minister's wife's new golf bag.
"Yes," she explained, "My husband got it for me when I caught him fooling around with our maid."
"Oh my God! Did you fire her?"
"No. I still need some new clubs."

'Why are you so late teeing off?'
"Its Sunday. I had to flip a coin between going to church or playing golf today."
"But why so late?"
"I had to flip it twenty times."

The minister interrupted his sermon to ask a man in the front row,

"Is my sermon boring you? Would you rather be out golfing?"

"No, why do you ask?"

"Maybe its that tight over-lapping grip you have on your hymnal."

The minister asked his young caddy how high he could count to.
The young man replied,

"Four."

"That's wonderful," said the minister.
"And what score did you give me on that last hole?"

"Two fours."

Reverend Bill blasted a sand wedge out of the trap and buried the ball
into an even deeper trap on the other side of the fairway. His lips pursed
intensely as he studied the errant ball. His caddy observed,

"Reverend, that's the most profane silence I have ever heard!"

A minister was playing golf in Italy. He was approaching a water trap on
the 12th hole and noticed a woman skinny-dipping in the pond. He turned
his head quickly and apologized saying,

"I'm so sorry. I must have taken you unawares."

To which she replied,

"Well, you just putta em back!"

Reverend Ike asked his caddy if he had any suggestions to improve the
reverend's shoddy game? The boy replied,

"You might try taking a month off."

"A good suggestion. The rest will certainly help. Then what?"

"Then quit."

The minister asked his caddy why he kept looking at his watch?

"Its not a watch Reverend, it's a compass."

Our minister was complaining that his new playing partner was way too overbearing. He said the man wouldn't even concede three-inch putts.

"Wow! That really slows up the game. Were you in a rush to finish?'

"No. But it was those five extra strokes it cost me."

Our minister finally managed to knock seven stokes from his game. When asked how he had accomplished this improvement so quickly, he explained.

"I just stopped playing that dang last hole."

Knock. Knock.

Knock, Knock.

Who's there?

Amen.

Amen who?

Amen over my head here.

Knock. Knock.

Who's there?

Heaven.

Heaven who?

Heaven you had enough yet?

Knock. Knock.

Who's there?

Andy.

Andy who?

Andy all lived happily ever after.

Knock. Knock.

Who's There?

Saul.

Saul who?

Saul there is, there tain't no more.

CONCLUSION

"Make a joyful noise unto the Lord... and make it Laughter."